LIFE WITH THE AKESTER

A Story of Overcoming Grief and Learning to Savor the Good Times

By:
Steve Akley

Written, Illustrated and Published by:
Steve Akley

Text copyright © 2013 Steve Akley
All Rights Reserved

Cover Design © 2013 Mark Hansen
All Rights Reserved

Illustrations © 2013 Steve Akley
All Rights Reserved

To Amy, Cat, Mom and Kelly:

We have lived this adventure together!

Lawrence E. Akley
1942 - 2012

Introduction

Buddies for Life – Larry "Akester" Akley and Steve (the author) in March 1968

While the root of Life with the Akester may be about my father, this book is much more than just his story. This is a journey through the depths of grief as well as insight into my personal recovery process. While I would be the first to admit, there is no instruction manual to ease the pain of the loss of a loved one, I believe seeing the path of another has gone through can be beneficial, so I am sharing my the story of coping with the loss of my father with you.

In the book, I speak of not moving on without a loved one, but accepting your new "normal." In the face of a sudden death, it is often stated that you need to go on and live your life because that's what your departed loved one would have wanted. I think everyone is inclined to agree, but it can be emotionally difficult to achieve.

In the first part of the book, we follow through my personal struggles and look at how I came to balance keeping the memories of my father alive while finding out to go beyond just living life and starting to experience joy again... something I had an incredibly difficult time grasping in the first months after his death.

After all, how could I have fun when he was dead?

My acceptance of "my new normal" is an interesting one; and it is my hope that if you are going through the loss of a loved one, it will be of some benefit to see the process I went through.

One of the things my dad instilled in me from a young age was to have fun, even if it was laughing at yourself. He enjoyed laughter so much and I would be remiss to write a book about him and not incorporate the funny stories we used to laugh about.

Part Two of the book is filled with thirteen laugh-out-loud stories from his life. He had so many funny situations happen to him over the years, it's almost unbelievable. I started writing them down a few years back. Anytime we wanted a good laugh, we would rehash the classics.

I always said I was going to put them in a book. I am sure he's looking down and laughing now that I am sharing them with the world.

While you didn't know my father, I am sure you will enjoy this look at *Life with the Akester*!

Table of Contents

Larry "Akester" Akley 9

Part I 17

Chapter One: Axe Grinders 18

Chapter Two: 12-12-12 20

Chapter Three: London 22

Chapter Four: The Duck Room 25

Chapter Five: Making Amends 43

Chapter Six: Chuck Berry 45

Chapter Seven: Dick Dale, King of the Surf Guitar 55

Chapter Eight: The Show 62

Epilogue Part I 68

The Beast 72

Part II 73

Chapter Nine: The Recorder 78

Chapter Ten: The Letter 81

Chapter Eleven: The Bowtie 84

Chapter Twelve: The Steps 90

Chapter Thirteen: The A++++ 95

Chapter Fourteen: The Dash 97

Chapter Fifteen: The Stories 100

Chapter Sixteen: The Encounter 104

Chapter Seventeen: The Roll 108

Chapter Eighteen: The Sandwich 112

Chapter Nineteen: The Bathroom 114

Chapter Twenty: The Singer	117
Chapter Twenty-One: The Chapstick	119
Epilogue Part II	121
Conclusion	123
Photo Album	127
Author's Notes	137
Index	141
Bonus Content	143
Special Thanks	147
Bibliography/Sources	148
Additional Resources	150
About the Author	152
Meet Team Akley	153
Also by Steve Akley	154

Larry "Akester" Akley
The Foundation

While this isn't a biography of my dad, it is a story about his life, his death, the overcoming of grief surrounding his sudden death, as well as a celebration of his life by sharing some of the funny stories we experienced with him over the years. Before we get to the heart of the book, I would like to share a bit of the back story… a look at my father's childhood and how it helped establish who he was a person.

Lawrence Edward Akley was born on August 20, 1942, to Lawrence Rile and Flora Akley. His father was a streetcar driver and his mother a homemaker. My dad always liked to say that looking back on his up-bringing, he would realize his family would be considered poor by today's standards. They just didn't realize it at the time. He would always note, "When everyone around you is in the same situation, it just seems like that's how life is, and we didn't know any other way to live."

Growing up poor helped build the foundation of strength in many aspects of my father's life. For him personally, it gave him keen insight into many of the issues he would later have to deal with as a public servant (a policeman). He knew firsthand the challenges families have to deal with when they are just scraping by. He also witnessed being poor isn't an excuse to break the law or live without a sense of pride in your life. While his family might have had less than even the other families in the area (after all, they never had a car or TV growing up), they still had a sense of pride about their home and family. Their house was never rundown, nor were they anything less than happy in the life they were living. They were simply hard working folks trying to get by.

Another key aspect engrained into my father was honesty. There is no better showcasing of this virtue than my dad's Steak 'n Shake glass story. My dad's father, Lawrence Akley (my dad was called Larry to his dad's Lawrence to avoid confusion) was an honest man to a fault. He had zero tolerance for anything less than 100% truthfulness. He also didn't use his financial situation as an excuse to break the law. Following the law and respect authority were mantras that he lived by.

When my dad was a teenager he and his buddies would enjoy the drive-up service at Steak 'n Shake. This was back when there were car hops to bring the meal to your car. They would bring out the burgers, fries and drinks in glass glasses (like you still find if you eat inside a Steak 'n Shake restaurant today), unlike the paper cups we would now associate with fast food drinks which are utilized by the few restaurants that still offer car service.

Many times after the meal dad and his buddies would hand the tray back to the car hop but keep their drinks in those cool Steak 'n Shake logo glasses. While it wasn't their policy to do this, it was commonplace, and they really weren't hiding it from the car hop when they did it.

One day my dad, his father and his mother were having dinner. His mother set those glasses on the table. My grandfather picked up one of the Steak 'n Shake glasses and asked, "Where did we get these?"

My father chimed in, "I got them at Steak 'n Shake. When you get the car service, sometimes we aren't finished with our drinks so we just keep them."

My grandfather comes back, "So you stole these?"

My father, on his heels, "No, I didn't steal them. They don't care. We just tell the car hop we're taking them. They never say a word. They really don't care."

My grandfather wasn't having any of this. "Is it posted you can keep the glasses if you buy a drink?"

My dad responded, "No."

My grandfather, going for the close, "Did you pay for them?"

Dad realizing where this is now going to go, "No."

"So you did steal them. Well, after dinner, wash these glasses, collect any others in the house and you will return them," my grandfather sternly responded.

For my dad, this wasn't a bad conclusion. He had no problem with gathering up the glasses and taking them out of the house. In his mind, he already had his plan of how it would play out. He'd leave, drop them off at a friend's house, never take another Steak 'n Shake glass, and it would be the end of the story.

Lesson learned.

"By the way," my grandfather added, "I want to be sure these get returned. I will be going with you to Steak 'n Shake when you return these glasses."

D'oh!

There goes my dad's plan. He put together a full-on protest. There was no way he was going to go to a Steak 'n Shake with his father to return those glasses. Ultimately, he lost the battle, though. For his dad, it was stealing and he simply could not have lived with himself had he allowed it.

After dinner, they washed the glasses, boxed them up and headed to Steak 'n Shake. When they arrived, my dad, with his father in tow went into the store and asked for the manager. This had to be quite the scene when you consider my dad wasn't eight at the time. He was a seventeen-year-old. Certainly still a kid, but not what you typically think of when you are imagining a child getting a life lesson about shoplifting from a parent.

My dad explained to him the manager how sometimes he didn't give the glasses back when he got car hop service and he was returning them. "He stole them," my grandfather interjected. My dad apologized (also part of my grandfather's instructions on making amends) and handed over the box of glasses to the stunned, and confused, manager.

My dad continued to go to Steak 'n Shake. He even enjoyed car service, but he never "stole" one of those glasses again!

It was this solid foundation which really set his career path. From a very young age, even before "glass-gate," he knew he wanted to be a policeman. It offered him a chance to not only rise above the life he had as a child, but also he saw it as a position of authority and a way to help others. It truly was a calling for him.

The other constant in my dad's life was the incorporation of humor and storytelling. He was always about enjoying the fun moments in life, even if they aren't fun at the time, and rehashing them.

Two of my favorite stories from his childhood are ones in which he got into trouble. As a kid myself, it was always endearing to hear about dad getting in trouble when he was my age (after the aforementioned Steak 'n Shake incident of course). One he kinda got away with and the other he incurred the quick and swift justice of the 1940's… the belt.

He always said as a young child the two times he got in the most trouble were when he lit the house on fire and he hit his dad in the head with a shoe.

With he was "burnin' down the house," it was the usual story of a kid playing with matches. He started a blaze which soon was out of control for him. Luckily, his parents were home and they got it under control without him burning the place to the ground. He loved the fact that while he got in trouble for that one, he avoided most of the wrath by hiding. His dad could immediately deal with him as it happened because he had to tend to the fire.

That window of chaos gave my dad his chance to escape and he took advantage of it. He actually hid under a chair in the living room. He stayed holed up for over 12 hours. No food, no bathroom, just a man and his thoughts. Child solitary confinement.

Of course my grandfather, my grandmother and other family members were searching for him. They do a sweep of the house and a hard-target search around the neighborhood but didn't find him. Had he answered their calls, he always claimed he had no doubt he would have been dealt with swiftly and severely.

By the time he emerged from his self-sentenced solitary confinement, the edge was off of the anger. My grandfather was just glad to see him. He realized it was a kid being a kid and while he had a stern talk with my him, dad avoided the belt… which is the kid equivalent of getting a call from the governor after they have already strapped you in to the electric chair.

The outcome wasn't as rosy in the other childhood story he liked to tell. His father was coming down on him pretty hard about his school work, grades and attitude in general. Like most kids he really didn't want to hear it. As the lecture went on-and-on, he started to become openly agitated with my grandfather's lecture. This building anger wasn't causing my grandfather to back off of the tongue-lashing, so my dad thought he would make a gesture which really showed him he was at the breaking point.

At the time dad, was wearing a pair of slip-on loafers. He thought he could really emphasize the point of "I've had enough" by kicking off one of those loafers to accentuate the point. So he yells, "Dad, I'm tired of hearing this" and goes to "kick off" a shoe. He really put some "umph" into it. After all, clearly the old man would be taken aback to see the passion of a loafer flying across the backyard, right?

Well, he kicked that loafer off just as planned. He hit the mark in terms of punctuating the point. The problem was in this attempt to really send this thing sailing, he held the toes a little too long before releasing the loafer off to the vast expanse of the backyard.

This totally changed the trajectory of the shoe and altered the course of Akley family lore forever. Rather than the triumph of a point well made, and accented by a flying loafer, that shoe made a direct line right to my grandfather.

Rather than getting the point of a well-timed statement, he took the point of a penny loafer right in the temple. There was no time to make this one right/nor any further points to be made here. My dad realized it was time to follow his successful strategy of the house fire incident and shag out of there.

Kick to the head aside, my grandfather wasn't preoccupied with putting out a potential devastating fire this time, though.

His only focus right then and there was to capture the perpetrator who not only defied him but had also just assaulted him. So he immediately jumped into action.

I wish I could say Larry ran to the safety of another chair, but the belt of justice caught up with him that day. His capture, trial and punishment were all conducted right there at that moment in the backyard. He was found guilty on all counts and dealt with accordingly.

Even though he lost his own father right after his high school graduation, he continued to profess the lessons he learned from his dad for the rest of his life. He maintained honesty, commitment to family and a keen sense of humor as the foundation of who he was.

He did also grow up to realize his dream of being a policeman. He had the admiration, respect and love from his family, friends and peers. He truly had a dream life (more on that later).

Part I

TWO NIGHTS IN THE DUCK ROOM

A Look at How Two Concerts, in a Famous Venue Featuring a Couple of Guitar Legends, Helped a Son Cope with the Loss of his Father

Chapter One: Axe Grinders

I have always had an infatuation with the guitar. To me, it seemed in most bands it was the lead guitarist battling with the lead singer for supremacy within the band. The rest of group tends to fall into the shadows of the lead singer and/or the guitarist.

Take the bass player for instance. While there are certainly exceptions, like Flea from the Red Hot Chili Peppers, I think the standard bass player is a blue-collar job. Put on your hard hat, grab your lunch pail and go to work. Like they used to say on *Seinfeld*, "not that there is anything wrong with that." It's just that for the most part, the bassist typically lets the other members grab the spotlight. The late John Entwistle of The Who may represent best the prototype of the bass player. During the show, he was just playing his music. Not jumping around. Not "wind milling." Not spinning microphones. Just playing.

The drummers seem like they want attention and recognition, it's just that they are tucked-in behind all of the equipment. I think they lose a connection with the audience being behind a wall of drums.

That sets the stage for the debate of guitar player vs. lead singer.

Certainly the lead singer is often the face of the group. The person that gets the attention of the audience during every song. Dress and theatrics are all part of the repertoire for the lead singer.

The guitar player is grinding it out, though. Creating signature riffs which make a song instantly recognizable. Pumping out sound that makes you want to move around; dance; go a little faster on the treadmill.

Singing styles are unique to the individual so you can never really compare one lead singer to another. While variances in the style of play for guitar can lead to totally unique sounds, there is a basis of framework and commonality to guitar playing which does allow us to compare the likes of a Dick Dale, Jimi Hendrix, Stevie Ray Vaughn, Eric Clapton and B.B. King.

The greatest debates surrounding ranking rock legends always focus on the guitar. There is always room for discussion, but the semblance in the foundation allows for comparison of guitarist, even when they are playing in different genres/styles of music.

Between March and May of 2013, I was about to see two of the all-time legends to ever play the guitar. I would just need to survive a tragedy which hurt our family to the core to get there.

Chapter Two: 12-12-12

Wednesday, December 12, 2012.

The day seemed like so many others, but it would end like no other. In the middle of an uneventful workday, my father came to pick me up and took me to lunch. This was something we often did. Our conversation centered on the usual stuff: football, family and laughs.

My dad dropped me off back at work, and I waved as he pulled away. I had no way of knowing as I watched him smile and wave, as he always did, that it would be the last time that I would ever see him alive. I don't have any ink on my body, but I have to tell you, my mind is tattooed with the snippet of his blue car driving away on that day.

The next several hours were normal for him as well. He picked up my daughter Cat from school and took her home. He hadn't stated to either of us that he wasn't feeling well and neither of us felt there were any indicators of something wrong. My mom happened to be out doing some Christmas shopping with my aunt. She came home to find my dad passed out in a chair.

He had showered and shaved in preparation to go out with a few friends that evening. Initially she thought had fallen asleep after getting ready. When he wasn't responsive, she called 911.

Emergency responders got there quickly and did manage to revive him. He was conscious and speaking, but a second heart attack in the ambulance on the way to the hospital proved fatal.

The next hours, days, weeks and even months were a blur. Disbelief. Grief. Depression. It was like my life became the instructions on the back of a shampoo bottle: "rinse, lather, repeat." Then there is the fact that everything you manage to do is stamped with the milestone of "without dad." Christmas… first Christmas without dad. New Year's… first New Year's without dad. Favorite restaurant. First time going without dad.

Well wishers keep taking you back to that day. What is the answer to "how are you doing?" after something like this happens. Does someone want to hear, "pretty bad?", or how about, "For no reason I cried on the way into work today?"

On the evening of 12-12-12, I couldn't have imagined anything ever sounding fun again. Life stopped for my dad, and it was put on hold for our family as we grieved for someone taken from us far too soon.

Chapter Three: London

In the months that followed the events of 12-12-12, I found the grief from the loss of my father to be extremely difficult. I could not imagine I would ever know anything again beyond the pain I was feeling. Perhaps some of the continuing sadness just comes from the repetition of everyday living. Get up, go to work, answer "how are you doing," come home, eat dinner, talk to the family, go to bed with so many questions surrounding the death of my father still unanswered (Why did he have to die?, Could have I done something that day?, Is he in heaven?, etc.).

If you are going to live a healthy and productive life, at some point something breaks the chain. A change which gives you the ability to cope, while not dulling the love and grief you have experienced over the loss.

My initial relief came from an invitation for a business trip to London. I probably will never know how or why I got invited. I just know that the trip had been planned with my boss, his boss and another colleague, and I wasn't part of the group.

Whether it was acknowledgement for a job well done, evaluation of career development for me, a way to help an associate in a tough time, or a combination of all of the above, whatever the reason; I was invited on the trip. The best part was that it was going to help me incredibly in my job, and it was going to be fun too as I had never traveled anywhere outside of the U.S. other than visits to our neighbors in Canada and Mexico.

One evening, my colleague and I were dining in one of the many old, cool pubs in London. We were sitting at the bar and the bartender, a London transplant from South Africa asked us where we were from.

"St. Louis" we told her.

"Never heard of it," she said.

"We have the Gateway Arch. Our NFL football team even played in London last year."

"Nope," she reiterated.

"We are near Chicago, I said."

"Okay," she finally acknowledged, "I have heard of Chicago."

With that, the song *Roll Over Beethoven* came on.

"Hey," I enthusiastically chimed in, "we are from where this guy is from;" gesturing upwards to emphasize the fact I meant the music."

"He's from St. Louis," I stated, never mentioning whom 'he' was by name.

"Oh my God," she exclaimed, "you are from the same place as Chuck Berry!"

She went on, "That is so cool. The guy is a legend. I love all of his music."

Now I knew Chuck Berry is rock-and-roll royalty. He is a "musician's musician" in that legends of rock, like Keith Richards, idolize him. I understood the appreciation for his music certainly extended well beyond the U.S. Who knew a bartender who grew up in South Africa and had never even heard of St. Louis could be such a fan, though?

I informed her, "Did you know he is still alive?"

"He is," she looked surprised.

"Get this," I stated, "not only is he still alive. He still plays. In fact, he does a regular gig. There is this little club in the basement of this St. Louis institution of a restaurant called Blueberry Hill. Once-a-month for like the last 15 years he has played a show. It's just a small intimate place. The perfect setting to see a legend in action."

She was now almost giddy, "That is so unbelievable. How many times have you gone to see Chuck play there?"

Uh-oh. I didn't anticipate that question, but as soon as she started to ask it, I knew what was coming and I was crestfallen.

"Ummm, never," I sheepishly told her.

Chapter Four: The Duck Room

Blueberry Hill – Home of the Duck Room

In 1997, Blueberry Hill, a restaurant in the St. Louis suburb University City, opened a musical venue named the Duck Room in its basement. The name came from Chuck Berry's signature low-slung "duck dance" for which he is famous for performing in live shows. The décor in the room ranges from cartoon ducks like Donald and Daffy, to hunting decoys, to photos of its namesake sauntering across the stage. Chuck

Berry officially christened the club by performing the first show there.

Today, more than 15 years later, Blueberry Hill owner Joe Edwards still marvels at his intimate club where performers love to play in. Of course, building it was a challenge which Joe won't soon forget either.

Joe Edwards isn't your average restaurant owner. Yes, he does own a restaurant, but he's also a visionary, risk-taking entrepreneur and caretaker of the Delmar Loop neighborhood (or simply The Loop as many locals call it).

With a ponytail and jeans as the dress of choice, he might not look like the conventional business executive, but he is as savvy in real estate deals as Donald Trump. His opened Blueberry Hill in 1972 as a rock-n-roll joint with a large collection of… well, collections! The whole place is filled with collectibles of pop culture items.

In 1980, he was a founding member of an organization to revitalize the Delmar Loop area. In 1988 he drew interest to the area by starting the St. Louis Walk of Fame honoring famous St. Louisans with stars on sidewalks in the neighborhood. In 1995 he expanded his business interests by restoring and re-opening the Tivoli Theatre, a movie house originally opened in 1924. In 2000 he opened a 2,000 seat live concert venue called The Pageant. In 2003 he added the Pin-Up Bowl, a state of the art "retro" bowling alley. In 2009 he opened The Moonrise, a boutique hotel.

All of his investments and work has made the Delmar Loop area of St. Louis one of the premier places to visit. He continues to work to improve it with his next project being a streetcar trolley which connects The Loop with St. Louis Forest Park, one of the largest urban parks in the United States.

The Duck Room

Despite all of this success, the crowning jewel of everything he has accomplished may be the 300 seat Duck Room. Artists who play the room brag about the acoustics and audience enthusiasm at the events hosted there. To hear Joe tell the story, you realize what a spectacular undertaking this project was.

Says Joe, "When we started the project the building was over 85 years old. We wanted to add a music venue so the basement seemed like the perfect place. The building had an existing basement but it only had 7 ½' ceilings. I knew that to get the sound and sight lines right we we're going to have to make some major changes."

Those changes involved removing the floor in part of the restaurant and some load bearing walls. A bobcat was lowered in to the basement and the foundation was dug out to accommodate a 10' ceiling.

Joe continues, "The way it was configured you couldn't get the necessary equipment down there so we literally had to carry loads of dirt out by the bucketful. In the end we had exactly the layout we wanted and a very artist friendly venue. Bands not only like the look, the sound and the layout with the big stage, but there are other extras they really appreciate. There is a dressing room in back that includes a shower. There is a private entrance to the stage from the back. The Duck Room is like its own little world. It's right in the basement of this very crowded and popular restaurant, but we can still conduct business while the venue is being used because we soundproofed the room when we built it. These are the little things which make a big difference for our artists."

Enjoying the venue is something that artists seem to do. Grandmaster Flash, Jewel, Alanis Morisette, Joe Perry, Duran Duran and Johnny Winters are just a few of the big stars who have played there over the years. Annually, the Duck Room hosts about 150 – 175 live events. These events range from full sets, to mini events where the artists who are playing local 20,000 seat venues will do a small concert for a group of fans and host the local media to promote the upcoming show.

Edwards' relationship with Chuck Berry is unique. Joe states, "We actually met back in the '60s. We started to become friends in the '80s. It's just one of those things that happened. Chuck is usually pretty guarded so it took a long time for us to become close."

Over time, their friendship and trust continued to grow and when Joe opened up his new venue he named it after his buddy. While Joe built it, you could say that Chuck "owns it." Every month he plays live in the Duck Room which continues to be a must see event.

Joe says, "Chuck Berry at the Duck Room has reached national prominence as a performance. *Rolling Stone* has written it up more than once. Chuck performs with the energy of a man half his age. While he may tire out by the end of the show, you can see how he draws energy during the event from the crowd. We are already gearing up for Chuck's 200th live performance in the Duck Room slated for January of 2014."

With its intimate capacity, solid fan base of individuals who love the ability to sit arm's length from the performers and a list of big name artists, the Duck Room is incredibly successful.

While concerts had been a big part of our life prior to having our daughter, we had gotten away from going to them after she was born. It's just one of those things where your priorities change.

Now that she was a little older, and has her own social life, Amy and I had started to talk about going to some shows again. We simply hadn't decided to jump in just yet.

It is certainly one of these twists which makes this story so unique. The shows at the Duck Room are so successful they do not need to be on TV and the radio hawking upcoming events. It would take the shame of a bartender in London to get me to realize I was missing a real opportunity to see a a legend which would lead me to see both him and the King of the Surf Guitar Dick Dale.

Blueberry Hill Photo Album

Joe Edwards, owner of Blueberry Hill

Blueberry Hill's famous burger

The Piano Room

The Pacman Room

The St. Louis Room

The Pez Collection

Elvis memorabilia display case

Joe Edwards and Chuck Berry

Joe Edward's other properties in the Delmar Loop area

(Top left clockwise: The Pin-Up Bowl, the Tivoli Movie Theatre, the Moonrise Hotel and the Pageant live music venue)

Timeline of Joe Edward's Improvements /Additions to the Delmar Loop

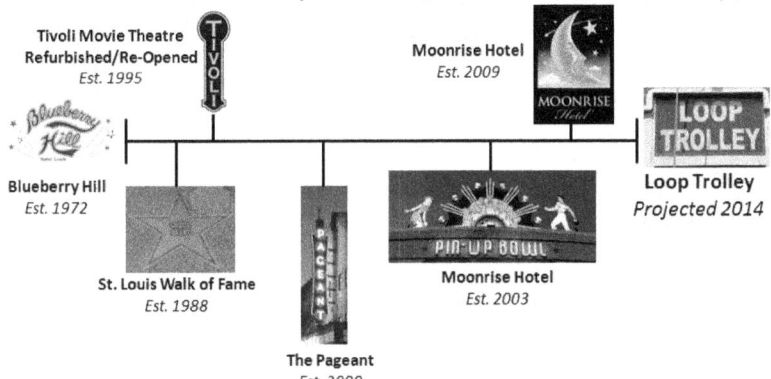

Tivoli Movie Theatre Refurbished/Re-Opened
Est. 1995

Moonrise Hotel
Est. 2009

Loop Trolley
Projected 2014

Blueberry Hill
Est. 1972

St. Louis Walk of Fame
Est. 1988

The Pageant
Est. 2000

Moonrise Hotel
Est. 2003

The Loop Trolley, Joe Edwards' next project

Chapter Five: Making Amends

The exchange with the bartender in London had been eye-opening. She was absolutely right. Chuck Berry is a guitar legend, who has influenced generations of guitarists, not just individuals.

Being from St. Louis, you almost take his legend for granted. Like many St. Louisans, seeing Chuck play live in the Duck Room at Blueberry Hill was on my list of things to do, but it always got put off when you factor in the frantic pace of day-to-day life with the fact he is so accessible (he plays *every* month after all, right?).

As that bartender stood in disbelief, I joined her in shock, and disappointment in myself. Chuck was already 86 years old.

Having lost my father just two months before, I began to immediately put together the finality of a missed opportunity. Right there, at a pub in London, I excused myself to call my wife Amy.

After exchanging the usual pleasantries, I told her to check Blueberry Hill's website (the restaurant with the Duck Room where Chuck plays every month) to see when the next time Chuck Berry played.

When she began to question it, I shut her down, "I've got to get back inside, just check when the next time he plays and let's be sure to get tickets. I want to go see Chuck Berry in the Duck Room. Cheerio." (You have to act like you are English when you go over there.)

The next time I spoke to my wife, she had the scoop. Tickets would go on sale in a few days (while I was still in England), and you had to buy them the moment they went on sale as they don't last long (The Duck Room has a capacity of 300).

"Pip, pip," I exuded, "that is jolly good news."

"Shut it with the accent," she scolded, "I will get the tickets."

Two days later I got the smashing word that she had been successful, and I would be going to see Chuck Berry in March.

She also had some other news, "When I was on the site buying the Chuck Berry tickets, I noticed they also were selling tickets for Dick Dale. Isn't he that guy you like who plays the song from *Pulp Fiction*?"

Now I was as excited as that London bartender, "Dick Dale is coming to the Duck Room? Are you kidding me? The guy is unbelievable. He plays the guitar like nobody else. Bloody hell, we gotta buy those tickets! Seriously, like as soon as we hang up, get us two for Dick Dale. *Miserlou*. The King of the Surf Guitar. Friend of Jimi Hendrix. *Pulp Fiction*. *Let's Go Trippin'*. *Pump It* by the Black Eyed Peas."

I'm not sure what happened there, I just lapsed into this Dick Dale giddiness where I started shouting out songs and phrases related to the guy.

I was walking on the clouds when I got a text from Amy about twenty minutes later confirming we had seats to see Dick Dale. Now I was set to see two guitar legends within about six weeks of each other!

Chapter Six: Chuck Berry

Wednesday, March 13, 2013.

That was the date I had tickets to see Chuck Berry playing in the Duck Room at Blueberry Hill. My wife, I, and 298 new friends would be experiencing an 86-year-old musical legend performing in a venue named after his celebrated "duck walk."

While I had been to Blueberry Hill, I hadn't been there for a show, just to eat. Since I didn't have any Duck Room experience, one thing I definitely took note of was the repeated warnings about very limited seating.

I did some quick math. You are to line-up 30 minutes to an hour before show time outside of the door to the Duck Room. Once they let you in, you have another hour until the opening act starts playing. The opening act then plays for an hour. You have about 15 minutes of turnaround time to get ready for Chuck and then he hits the stage and plays for at least an hour.

Let's see:

45 minutes + 60 minutes + 60 minutes + 15 minutes + 60 minutes x 45 year old feet/knees/hips and back = PAIN!

We had to be sure we were in position to score some of that coveted seating so we elected to arrive at 7:00 sharp.

Chuck Berry statue across from Blueberry Hill

As we arrived to the Delmar Loop where Blueberry Hill is located, you really get a feel for the impact Chuck has had on the area. There is a larger than life statue across from Blueberry Hill. Right outside of the restaurant he has a star which is part of the St. Louis Walk of Fame.

Chuck's star on the St. Louis Walk of Fame

Surprisingly, we managed to arrive right at 7:00 and proceeded to the Duck Room to stand in line. Initially, we were shocked as the line ran all the way through the dining room where the door was and down a long hallway filled with celebrity photos with Blueberry Hill owner Joe Edwards.

Ouch!

Could it be possible we might end up not getting a seat after all? That's ouch x 7 based on my math (2 knees/hips/feet + 1 back)!

During our hour while we were standing in line waiting for the Duck Room to open, it was enjoyable talking to our fellow fans. It was amazing how many had similar stories to ours. Something they always wanted to do and finally had the spark to be there that night. Right behind us we had two guys who drove five hours from Chicago just to be at the show. I told them they know all about Chicago in London!

About fifteen minutes before the doors to the Duck Room were slated to open up the club manager came out to greet everyone. He stated the show ends when Chuck is done playing. He emphasized that there was no set time, no guarantee about the number of songs, when Chuck stops playing, the show is over.

It might have seemed standoffish had it been a younger performer, but everyone seemed fine with the concept of an 86-year-old legend dictating when a night was over.

He also said that we would get the opportunity to meet Chuck after the show. "He does autograph items," he stated, "though he won't sign guitars."

Darn!

Opportunity lost. I didn't bring anything to get autographed. I was still going to stick around to meet him, though. That's a once in a lifetime opportunity I didn't want to miss, and it would make for a great keepsake if we could have someone in line snap a photo of Amy and me with my cell phone.

The doors opened about five minutes after 7:00. Right in front of the couple ahead of us, five people got stopped at the door. When asked where were their tickets they stated they didn't have any. They saw everyone "lining up to see Chuck Berry" so they got in line to see the show.

Honestly, who assumes they do not need a ticket for a show like this? I mean there were five of them. Couldn't four of them "hold the spot in line" while the fifth ventured out to the management at Blueberry Hill and found out about the ticket situation? Better yet, why not ask those around them? I mean we were standing there for an hour. Plenty of time to ask a person, or two, or ten!

This ended up being just the break Amy and I needed because when those five fell out of line (despite their protests about having had to wait so long) because they didn't have tickets, we were put up five spots further and that ended up being the difference between sitting for 3 hours or having to stand. When Amy and I got into the Duck Room, there were two seats together and two other separated seats left in the whole venue. We grabbed the two together. My feet/knees/hips and back thank those confused tourists who thought this was either a free show or something they could buy tickets for inside!

There are only four rows of chairs (approximately 100 of the 300 people get a seat). We were in the fourth row, on the aisle, just to the right of the stage. These were really great seats. Literally 15 feet from where Chuck Berry would soon be playing.

The opening band was great. They played covers of big hits from the 1960s. The most exciting part, though, was there was a flurry of activity to the right of the stage where the door leading to the back room stands. People were going in and out of that door as the opening act played on. I found myself paying more attention to the activity there than on the band.

The reason?

Well, I wanted to see Chuck Berry, of course!

I kept craning my neck to see around that open door every time someone opened it… and then one time, it opened wide and there sitting on the chair straight in from the door was the man himself. Unmistakable in his loose-fitting sparkled shirt and white captain's hat.

At that exact moment I couldn't begin to comprehend how good this show was going to be. I mean for God's sake, I was absolutely fascinated by the man sitting in a freakin' chair.

How could I even begin to ratchet that enthusiasm up even higher when the guy starts playing his guitar and all of those songs I've heard my whole life? Is there a possibility I was going to die tonight? I'm not talking heart attack either. I'm thinking some sort of not-yet-understood-by-science, spontaneous combustion. "Ladies and Gentlemen, Chuck Berry" …BOOM! Steve's gone!

The moments leading up to Chuck entering the stage are incredible. The opening act winds down and then there are the stage hands out testing mics and setting up equipment. You know he's about to come out, yet you don't entirely believe it is actually going to happen.

And then… there he is. Chuck Berry strolls through the door and immediately starts playing *Jambalaya*. I have to tell you, it is a rush of emotions. First, I can't believe he's there in the room. I'm not kidding when I say my brain stopped functioning for a while. Initially, I wasn't hearing him sing. I was paralyzed. Do I take a photo, scream, whistle, just kick back and enjoy the show?

Chuck Berry in the Duck Room: A legend takes the stage

I wouldn't say I would be the type who is prone to getting star struck. I tend to believe these individuals are people like you and me that just happen to have some sort of skill that makes us idolize them.

This was different, though. This is the same guy who has entertained millions. A star who is revered as a god by fellow musicians. Now, he's in this small room with me and a couple of hundred other fans.

Unbelievable!

There was also a moment where I got a little choked up. I started thinking about my father, and how I wish he was here for the show. He too was a fan and in the past we had even talked about to coming to Blueberry Hill to catch him.

I wasn't going to get emotional though. I wanted to enjoy the moment so I took a few deep breaths and listened to Chuck singing about "oh mi, oh my oh, he was going to have some fun on the buy-oh."

Then it's just one hit after another. The incredible licks in *Roll Over Beethoven*. The unique halting delivery in *School Day*. The haunting beat of *Maybelline* and many more. In between songs he's talking to the audience and having fun and asking if they have any requests. In the song *Back in the U.S.A.* he seemed like a 20-year-old as he was running side-to-side on the stage. The song even featured an awesome harmonica solo from his daughter.

He was so active during this song, I actually leaned over to Amy and said, "He's 86, how can he keep up this pace?" With that, he took a seat and played the next song in his chair. I don't think anyone thought twice about it. I mean the guy's 86!

He then got back up and played a couple more top hits. Between songs, people started yelling, "play *My Ding-A-Ling*," but I knew it wasn't meant to be when he kicked in with *Johnny B. Goode*. I had read online that's how he closes the show.

Sure enough, as soon as that song started, the people near the door started preparing for Chuck's exit. They removed anything from around the door and actually let it stay open. During the song he actually looked like he was heading out through the door. He then sat on a chair next to the door.

Finally, as the song was probably ¾ of the way complete, he headed back to the other side of the stage for a big guitar solo. The solo culminated with a signature "duck walk." Sure, he didn't get as low as I've seen him do in black-and-white photos from the old days, but the fact he could even do what he was doing made my meniscus hurt!

As the band finished the last notes of *Johnny B. Goode*, Chuck left the stage. No encores here, the band immediately started tearing down after Chuck's daughter introduced the band and his son thanked everyone for coming. Chuck did step out of the backroom to wave to the crowd.

What an unbelievable performance! This octogenarian had delivered a performance that had the audience eating out of the palm of his hand.

As the house lights began to come back up people started lining up on the stage. Oh yeah, Chuck signs autographs after the show!

Amy and I climbed up over some lighting and on to the stage to wait the opportunity to shake hands with a legend. I have to tell you the relationship between celebrities and fans is fascinating. Right in front of us was this 50ish woman in far too revealing of an outfit for her age. Chuck is certainly old enough to be a great-grandfather and even the father of this old piece of leather. Despite the advanced age of both star and fan, her plan, in her words was, "I'm going to have Chuck sign my tits!"

Alas, it was opportunity lost for all involved when the stage manager came out and informed us that Chuck was done signing for the night. There would be no handshake and photograph with a legend tonight for us, nor would there be any signed cans for Mae West. Apparently, the autograph line stops when Chuck is done signing!

That's all right, it was the perfect night and I left wondering when the *next* time I would be seeing Chuck playing in the Duck Room. Of course in a few short weeks I would be seeing one of the few people in the world you could argue is more influential than Chuck Berry. Dick Dale was scheduled to play the same venue on May 2.

Chapter Seven: Dick Dale, King of the Surf Guitar

Dick Dale Comes to the Duck Room

As great as the Chuck Berry show had been, I was even more enthused about going to see Dick Dale. Not meaning I was comparing the experience of one guitar legend vs. another. It's just that I had always *assumed* I would be going to see Chuck Berry, even if I didn't have immediate plans to do so.

Dick Dale was different. Despite the fact I am a huge fan of his music, I honestly would have never known about him coming to St. Louis had it not been for the discussion about Chuck Berry in London which spurred us to get off of our duffs and go see him in concert. Of course, my wife played a big role in this when she saw Dick Dale booked for the Duck Room when she was buying the Chuck Berry tickets. The Duck Room has its own following that means they don't have to promote it like the huge venues where they have to sell 20,000 tickets when an artist plays in St. Louis so I likely wouldn't have heard anything about Dick Dale's concert otherwise.

In full disclosure, I have to admit I was late to get onboard with his sound. You have to cut me some slack, though. I was born well over a decade after he created the genre of surf music, and I'm from St. Louis. We've got the Mississippi. You may see someone noodling for catfish in it, but you aren't going to see anyone surfing!

Miserlou

My introduction to Dick Dale came about like so many others in the second stage of his career: the movie *Pulp Fiction*. The first time I ever remember hearing Dick Dale play, or even his name, was connected to the fact his song *Miserlou* was featured as the opening for *Pulp Fiction*, and in its trailers and commercials. The sound of that song was like nothing I had ever heard before (or since). Those sharp notes, building, going faster until you think it's as fast as a human can possibly play; then it kicks into yet another faster gear.

Pulp Fiction is such a great movie it probably would have been a hit with or without *Miserlou*. Then again, you never know. The song seemed to be a precursor not only to the movie, but also the style of the movie: fast-paced and unique. At this point, the two are connected. You simply cannot hear that song come on and not think of *Miserlou*, and you can't think of *Pulp Fiction* without having that guitar sound pop into your head.

Fast-Paced Staccato

Any time you hear Dick Dale's guitar playing discussed, or read about him, his style is usually described as fast-paced staccato. Now I'm not a music tactician. I've never played any instrument, nor have I taken any type of class in music. I'm simply a fan of what I like. I don't even know what staccato is.

Sure, I can look it up in the dictionary and see it's a note of shortened duration, but I'm not exactly sure that tells me anything by itself. No, for me, Dick Dale is the definition of fast-paced staccato. If anyone mentions somebody else playing a "fast-paced staccato" I'm not using the brain to compare and contrast their musical work versus a dictionary definition of "a note of shortened duration." No way. Instead for me, my mind is going right to Dick Dale and comparing it to his music and his style of play. I am guessing for most artists, that's a rough place to go. I mean how can you stack up against one of the most legendary guitarists of all time?

The song *Miserlou* is so unbelievably different than anything I had ever heard so I have to admit I initially thought it was some sort of studio trick. Was the music sped up in studio? Were different tracks stitched together so you can find another gear beyond "breakneck" pace?

The invention of *YouTube*™ allowed me to see Dick Dale live playing his "fast-paced staccato" style. The best part, *Miserlou* is not only 100% authentic, the live version sounds every bit as good as, if not better than, the studio cut.

Equipment Used by Dick Dale

That unique sound comes from equipment which is now tried and true. Like most great musicians, Dick Dale is extremely particular about his guitars and amps. He uses a vintage Fender Stratocaster he calls, "The Beast." The amps he uses are a story themselves. The equipment of the 50's wasn't quite ready for a "fast-paced staccato" genius wailing on "The Beast." He kept blowing out his amps. Leo Fender himself came to a show to see what was happening and designed a new piece of equipment to handle the sound coming from the likes of a Dick Dale. The Showman Amp (named after Dick and his "showman" stage presence) was born.

Dick Dale is Crowned King

The unprecedented sound Dale could produce via his Fender Stratocaster and Showman Amp led *Guitar Player* magazine to deem him the "Father of Heavy Metal."

While flattered by the recognition, Dale prefers the moniker, "King of the Surf Guitar." After all, it's an homage to the unique genre of music he created all the way back in the 1950's, surf music. The recreation of the sounds, pace and feel of surfing in the ocean via music played by the guitar. Sound difficult to do? Well don't worry, Dick Dale invented it and when you listen to it, you just have to agree… it's surf music.

Dick's preferred nickname actually came from real surfers. In California in the early days of his career you had to get a license to play live rock-and-roll music at dance halls. Bands with guitars were not receiving permits but Dick Dale successfully petitioned to get a license with the opening of the Rendezvous Ballroom. His rationale being, "was it better to have the kids in one place, entertained, or out on the streets doing who knows what."

He was approved with one requested concession. The males attending would have to wear a tie. Dick agreed and the show was on!

There was quite a scene at the actual event with the surfers in attendance. Many of them were walking around with bare feet. Shoeless or not though, everyone was in a tie, with the band having distributed them for those who didn't bring one.

His nickname was born that night as the surfers in attendance kept saying, "man, you are the king!" From that point forward, Dick Dale became the King of the Surf Guitar.

Taking Control of His Career

By anyone's calculation Dick Dale has had a helluva career. Not only is he credited with creating surf music and metal, he's got the respect and admiration of his fellow musicians and a strong base of devoted fans. It does leave you to wonder why he isn't as well known as someone like Keith Richards, Eric Clapton, Pete Townshend or any of his other guitar virtuoso contemporaries.

His early career was highlighted with a conventional approach to the music business. He signed with Capitol Records™. He had appearances on the *Ed Sullivan Show* as well as in multiple surf/beach movies with Annette Funicello and Frankie Avalon.

Despite the success of following the carved path of an established musician, Dale realized the many pitfalls of working through a label. The problems he identifies include the loss of control of your music. The inability to establish and control your own brand and image. There is also the matter of money. With a label, you get a nice stipend upfront, but it is at a cost of a much lower return from that point forward. Today, he professes a path of an artist maintaining control of his or her music. He's a solid believer in creating and distributing your own music by building up a fan base and keeping control of your career and your product.

Keeping control of your career is a mantra that Dick Dale lives by today. He's doesn't have a manager, a booking agent or a company handling his public relations. He negotiates his own deals, books his shows and has complete control of his music. He even hosts and maintains his own website, personally responding to emails. With his music, he's grinding it out at shows, connecting directly with a fan base to which he adds to with each show, staying on well after it ends to sign autographs.

The Life of a Legend

Taking control of his own career was only one of the challenges Dick faced in his lifetime. In 1964 he was diagnosed with rectal cancer and at that point given only 3 months to live.

Utilizing a laser for surgery, at that time a state-of-the-art experimental procedure, Dick Dale did recover and was cancer-free until it returned in 2008. He ended up having chemo, radiation, surgery to remove the tumors as well as reconstructive surgery. With his health returned, he once again resumed a full complement of shows.

Two Legends/One Friendship

His bout with cancer in the 1960's opened up the world to his relationship with Jimi Hendrix. Dick Dale met Hendrix when Jimi was playing in Little Richard's band. They bonded over discussions about new sounds with the electric guitar. At the end of his song *Third Stone from the Sun*, Jimi speaks the line "we'll never hear surf music again" as a tribute to his mentor Dick Dale who was still ailing at the time. While some, unfamiliar with the relationship of the two musicians, wondered if that was some sort of jab at the surf music sound. The opposite was true. Jimi truly meant this as words of encouragement for someone whom he looked up to as an artist. Dick relishes their relationship to this day often sharing what a great guy Jimi was until he started using drugs. He recorded his own version of *Third Stone from the Sun* as a tribute back to Jimi and often plays it in concert.

Dick Dale Today

At age 76, Dick Dale no longer surfs, though he does remain active. He stopped when he almost lost his leg from an infection caused by a cut he got while surfing in polluted water. Today he keeps his surfing limited to the sound he creates on the guitar.

He does continue to keep an aggressive touring schedule. He is often joined on stage by his son Jimmy who matches his father's fast-paced guitar playing with his own hectic-paced drumming. He started playing with Dick onstage by the time he was five. Today, he is an accomplished musician who also plays bass and guitar.

Dick is a proud member of both the Surfer's Walk of Fame in Huntington Beach, Calif. and the Musician's Hall of Fame in Nashville, Tenn.

Chapter Eight: The Show

Thursday, May 2, 2013.

After a quick bite to eat as soon as we got home from work, Amy and I headed straight to Blueberry Hill. We wanted to get there early to once again ensure we had seats to the show. As soon as we arrived, we knew we were in good shape… we were the third couple in line!

Time seemed to go by quickly during the hour-long wait as we were talking with the other fans about Dick Dale and other shows we had been to in the Duck Room as well as other venues. The doors opened, and we filed down the steps to the Duck Room. This time we didn't have to worry about getting a chair, in fact we ended up in the front row!

The opening act was good, but the crowd truly was there to see Dick Dale, and you could feel the excitement building in the wait between them finishing and turning over the stage. By the time the stage was ready to go, it was almost to a frenzy level. Each time the doors from the Green Room opened, everybody was on the edge of their seats anticipating the band walking through the door. There would be extreme disappointment as it would be one of the stagehands bringing out a piece of another instrument or tweaking some of the equipment. Of course, a few people are trying to get the chant going, "We want Dick… we want Dick" much to the amusement of other guests.

Finally, everybody is sitting in anticipation and a guitar note blasts through the speakers. The term "blast" is an understatement, mind you. I mean I nearly jumped through the back brick wall of the Duck Room from my front row seat as that note hit. It was just such a surprise since the Green Room door was closed, and no one was onstage.

At that, the door opened and the drummer and bass player walk out. No Dick yet, but he has now started playing the song *Nitro* from backstage and the bass player and drummer are playing on stage… and out he walks.

DICK FREAKIN' DALE!

Just like with Chuck Berry, it's a surreal moment. The moment of seeing a legend, still at the top of his game at 75 (he would turn 76 two days later), is taken to an unbelievable strata by the venue. Again, hats off to Joe Edwards of Blueberry Hill for his vision with the Duck Room. I am literally staring face-to-face from 4 feet away in the front row at a rock legend… and the guy is rocking. The sound is loud, but it is clear and the band is playing tight. The drummer is smacking the skins with reckless abandon. The bass player is ripping off riffs, and Dick Dale is just shredding it.

As *Nitro* ends Dick talks to the crowd, and he will continue to do that through the course of the evening. It seems he literally engages everyone in the immediate area. He even gave me a nod of acknowledgement during a fist pump!

He shared some funny, interesting and touching stories during the course of the event. *Esperanza* seemed to be a personal favorite as he set it up by talking about the aphrodisiac qualities of the song on the women. (I will have to remember to keep that one on the playlist on special nights!)

He also talked about how he made a side trip just that morning down to Memphis to record a song at historic Sun Studios. He then dedicated the song to military veterans, firefighters and the police… which for me had a special bit of meaning since Dad had loved his time with the St. Louis Police Department so much. The song was a very respectful, but slightly amped up version of *Amazing Grace* with a twist of rock-and-roll. It wasn't just a cover of it, he definitely Dick "Dale-ized" the song. Very cool. He mentioned that it was a true bucket list item for him recording a song where Elvis, Johnny Cash, Jerry Lee Lewis, Carl Perkins and so many others stars made names for themselves at.

He ended up playing all of his favorites like *Let's Go Trippin'*, *Hava Nagila*, *Pipeline* and then a bunch of awesome covers like *Ring of Fire* and *Ghost Riders in the Sky*.

He talked about how he doesn't do set lists or work with the band beforehand on what they are going to play. It's all about the feel of the moment. From the friendly confines of the Duck Room, you get to see all of this going down. I was literally able to watch Dick directing the band like a field general just with the most subtle of cues to let them know what to do. It just added to the whole cool factor of the entire event.

In addition to the guitar, he also played the harmonica, drums and even the bass. His turn on the bass was really unique in that he played the bass using drum sticks to strike, tap and stroke out a song. I can't say I've ever seen that done before, but it worked extremely well and was also an impressive audio and visual performance to witness.

He ended the night with *Miserlou*. I have always told the story of my all-time favorite concert moment which had been the song *Live and Let Die* when Paul McCartney came to St. Louis and played Busch Stadium with Wings. It was the combination of his legendary status, a great song, and a light show which enhanced the chaos of the musical interlude between verses that just really made that moment within the concert my all-time favorite.

I have to tell you, with Dick Dale and *Miserlou*, a new standard has been set. I got goose bumps when that thick guitar sound wailing out of "The Beast" delivered those opening notes. You literally know that song in one note, it's unbelievable. Here I am, watching in awe, from four feet away at a guy wailing on a guitar, playing so quick, so cool and so awesome, it's unbelievable. Then you get to thinking, this guy playing the guitar four feet away is the same dude who captured the imagination and had such an impact on a young Jimi Hendrix.

Powerful!

Dick is hitting every note, doing the dance from *Pulp Fiction*, emphasizing the song with the "heys" from the song. Then, as when he gets to the point in *Miserlou* where you think it's as fast as a human can possibly play, he introduces you the "other" gear that seems beyond the realm of human capability. Perhaps that is the line between guitar player and guitar god!

After the show ends, his wife Lana worked the merchandise table. I saw a great shirt I really wanted, but Lana had to really go digging for it for me, and she was able to find an XXL. I am happy to say am a proud owner of a blue long-sleeve t-shirt with a surf board crossing "The Beast" and Dick Dale running down the arm.

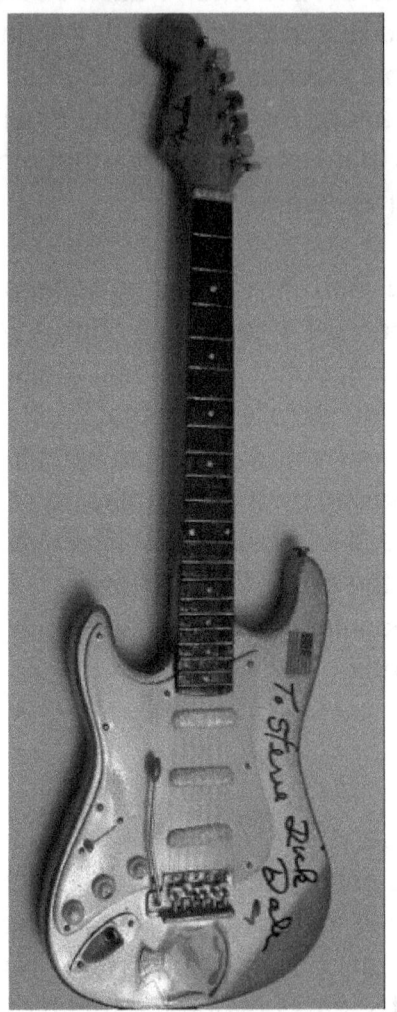

*The mini version of "The Beast"
Dick Dale autographed for me*

In an evening where you don't think things could get any better, they were just about to, in fact, ascend to even greater heights. Dick came walking back from the Green Room and joined Lana at the merchandise table. They shared a warm kiss, and he sat down to hang with the fans. I brought with me a poster, a drawing I did, and a mini version of "The Beast" for Dick to sign. He graciously did and then shook my hand.

What an evening!

I saw the greatest show of my life. I experienced the best "concert moment" in all of the concerts I have attended, and I got to meet the lovely Lana Dale and the King of the Surf Guitar Dick Dale!

My journey had brought me to this moment where I could officially say I can start to experience joy, create fond memories even when dealing with the emotional grief of losing someone I cared so deeply about.

Epilogue Part I

So seeing a couple of guitar legends live in concert managed to heal the grief I had incurred over the loss of my father?

That would be a great story, but in reality it hasn't happened. Not even close. My dad was a constant in my life and I never began to emotionally consider the impact of life without him. While he had some health issues in the last few years, he was too "full of life," and didn't have any problems where his death seemed eminent, so life without him seemed like something we would be dealing with in the distant future.

To his credit, he lived his life like he wanted to live it to the day he died. That's the sadness and tragedy of a heart attack. There may be minimal suffering for the individual, but the loved ones left behind are left to deal with the loss without the opportunity to say goodbye, or, in cases like ours, prepare themselves to even think it could happen.

What these shows actually did for me was to show me you can begin to have fun again. Enjoy yourself. Create unique memories even though your loved one is gone.

Like everyone who loses a parent, I had to figure out how to go on with my life. I have a family. A wife and daughter who need their husband and father. A mother who needed my emotional support. My job, where my co-workers and bosses need me continuing to perform my "duties as assigned." My creditors who need me to pay my bills. You simply can't wallow in grief; even as your mind may be screaming for you to do so.

In the months that followed the loss of my father, I think I managed to cope and continue "living my life," but what was missing was the ability to have fun, laugh and create great memories as we always did when dad was alive. From an outsider's perspective, in the months following my dad's death, it may have looked like I was getting by pretty well. I managed to continue going to work and interacted normally with co-workers. I had my moments where I was overcome with grief, but managed to hide them from friends and the individuals I worked with.

Looking back, I was really just grinding out life each day, waking up and doing it again the next. The thought of trying to do anything fun was met with disdain and guilt. Despite the fact I knew that clearly dad would want everyone to go on, I kept going back to the thoughts of "Dad's not here."

The trip to London was the start of the recovery, but the real key was the conversation with the bartender about Chuck Berry. Finally realizing that you can't continue to put off something you could so easily do was eye-opening.

So while seeing Chuck Berry and Dick Dale wasn't the key to moving on after the death of my father, it did show me that you can still have fun, while not reducing the sense of loss over a loved one.

The truth was I got to go to the two greatest shows of my life. Afterwards, I still felt the pain of the loss of my dad, but I also had these great memories from these two unbelievable performances. In my new reality, that actually felt pretty great. What I mean is that I didn't want to reduce the sense of loss and grief over the death of my father. Prior to these shows, I was worried if I moved forward in anyway, I had this strange sense that the love for my father would begin to dim.

The three greatest pieces of wisdom I can share from this experience are as follows:

1). Love your family with all of your heart and never simply go through the motions of everyday life. Relish the memories and time you have together because you truly never know when it may end.

2). Don't miss out on unique experiences in life just because you are "too busy." Find a way to make them happen. Don't keep putting off that unique experience because you may miss your chance to do so.

3). When dealing with the grief over the loss of a loved one, don't put any sort of expectations or timetables to deal with your loss. It is a process each person needs to handle individually. Look for the love and support from friends, family and your church to help out, but deal with the pain on your own terms in your own way.

Thanks to my dad, who along with my mom, taught me everything I needed to know about life. Their love and support went beyond raising me; they were a constant resource of knowledge that I drew upon until the day my father died and continue to do so with my mother.

In dealing with grief, I do not like the phrases "letting go" and "moving on." In my mind there is a connotation that the grieving process is over and things are back to normal. That simply cannot be the case. Life has changed for the Akley family forever. There never will be a time when I don't miss my father and yearn to have him back with us. Bringing back the emotions of fun and joy, though, has been great so I thank Chuck Berry and Dick Dale for reminding me, there is more to life than sadness and grief.

You can still love your lost family member, still grieve for them, while enjoying the new moments life brings you.

The Beast
(Steve's "Frankenstein Version")

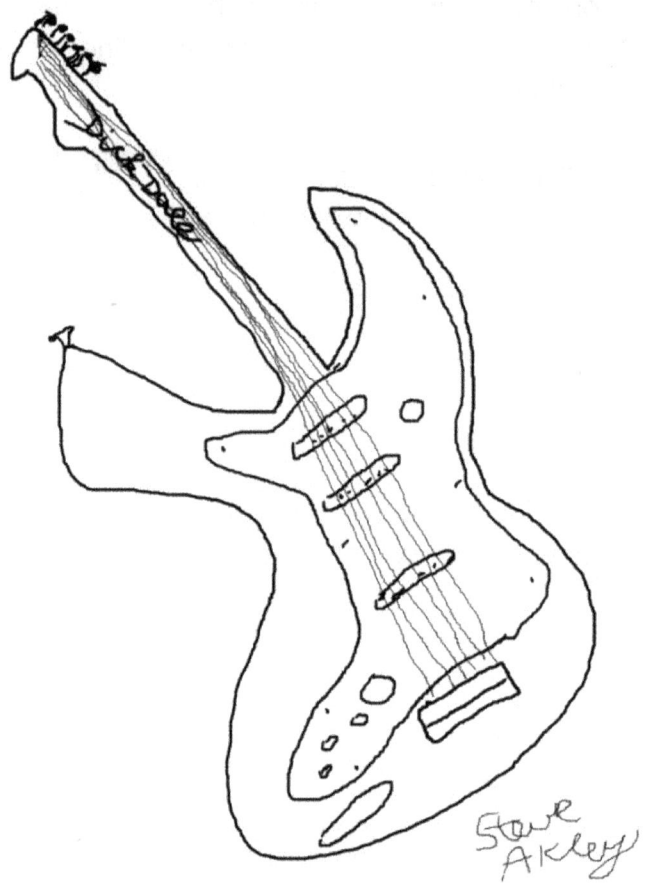

Part II

LAUGHING WITH THE AKESTER

A Baker's Dozen of Unbelievably Funny Stories from the Life of My Father

Introduction Part II

Dad at Yellowstone in 2011

Public Service Announcement

First off, if you read the stories in this section of the book on after another you are making a mistake. It is meant to be savored and enjoyed. It's like how a fine meal is served in courses versus a crappy buffet where you just pile everything together. Take your time, read it a story at a time, rehash it with friends/coworkers and your Facebook account. Then read the next one. Better yet, at a party, assign the person who can't control his or her laughter the job of reading a story aloud. Whenever that person starts to laugh, remind them to take the job of reading seriously! If you take this approach, you will get the full experience of the book.

Now, on with the regularly scheduled program…

Lawrence E. Akley.

That's the name *most* of the world knew my dad by. To the family though, he was the Akester.

Honestly, it often seemed like Lawrence E. Akley and the Akester were two very different people. There was a common thread that both Lawrence E. Akley and the Akester were incredible individuals who were beloved by those around them… yet very different indeed.

Lawrence E. Akley had an incredible life. He grew up poor in St. Louis but he had a dream to become a policeman. As a young man, he achieved his dream while getting married and raising a boy and girl. His career was perfect. He loved the police department and rose through the ranks quickly. As he closed in on retirement, he landed a job as the top official, building the dome where the St. Louis Rams would eventually play. Upon completion of that job he finished out his career as an executive of a local company.

Without fail, at each step of his career, he was beyond admired. I think it would be safe to say that he was cherished. Growing up poor and working his way through the ranks of the police department built a foundation which kept him humble wherever he was working… no matter at which level he was in an organization. It was this common-man approach which connected with those around him.

When he died suddenly on December 12, 2012, the line at his wake went out the door when the funeral parlor opened and stayed that way the whole time. Each person sharing how much he meant to them on a personal level.

The Akester?

Well, that was a different story entirely. Don't get me wrong. My dad was the ultimate father. The type of dad who would do anything for you, a guy you could always turn to for advice, and a person who loved his family above and beyond anything else. It was just that he was kind of a mess in his personal life.

The same guy, who was making critical life-and-death decisions on the police department, or million dollar decisions in the corporate world, seemingly was confused in the civilian life. Of course, the confusing thing for the family, was that fact that he too was a civilian!

It often felt like all of the pressures, decisions and politics of a career meant he shut all of that down in his personal life and he just lived. Of course, his approach often left those very love ones scratching our collective heads at some of the unbelievable stuff he did.

I'm not kidding here. My dad did some of the craziest stuff I have ever seen. Not like a one-time thing. I mean all of the time. Eventually, I realized we had an untapped goldmine and started writing some of these stories down. At family gatherings I'd pull out the laptop and make my wife read them. The best part about having her do it is that she could never make it through the story without tears running down her face as she gasped for air trying to read through the laugher as we all relived these memories.

Some of you may wonder if my dad would be okay with us sharing these stories. We always said we were putting them in a book, and he's sat through multiple readings of each. Sometimes he'd attempt to defend himself, but inevitably, he'd give up and just join in the laughter with us. None of this ever tabled his hijinks mind you. Despite the humiliation of hearing the family laughing at him, he was just as likely do something crazy again the next week.

For the book we've pared it down to his best stories. His "greatest hits," if you will. As such, you get to enjoy nothing but his truly funniest moments.

I hope you enjoy reading them as much as we enjoyed *living* them!

Chapter Nine: The Recorder

Oddly, my favorite Christmas memory doesn't come from any number of the blessed things I've experienced in my life, but more along the lines of the quirky, offbeat things which build the character of whom you are as a person.

In 1978, the 10-year old version of me only wanted one thing for Christmas: a tape recorder. Looking back now, I'm not exactly sure why that was, but at that moment in time, it was the only thing I cared about. I realize it's laughable now, but in 1978, this was cutting edge "in-home" technology. No longer was the recording of voices limited to the celebrity likes of Lee Majors; a person could actually record his or her own voice without going to a studio.

Christmas morning came and I opened up the new jeans, socks, dress shirts and other things Mom would wrap to increase the volume of gifts. She was smart enough to strategically bury the good stuff deep under the tree, so you continue to mow through all of it as she took photos of the ever disappointed reactions to these motherly gems.

My last gift was my beloved tape recorder. I wasn't allowed to simply take it off on my own and play with it. My dad had me run through the instruction book with him. To record, hit the record button. To play back your tape, hit play. Rewind involved pressing the rewind button. Pretty standard stuff. Dad and I were ready to proceed with our initial recording session.

My dad pressed the record button, picked up the recorder and spoke directly into the machine. Slowly and deliberately he dictated the inaugural recording. He said, "What are you doing?"... only he didn't say it in his own voice. He used robot-like voice and paused after each word with his voice pitch rising on the last word so it became, "WHAT .... ARE ... YOU ... dooo-ING?" I'm not sure why he chose this robot-like voice; perhaps he felt you needed to speak in what he considered a futuristic sounding voice with such new age technology.

He rewound the tape, and we heard robot man speaking back to us: "WHAT .... ARE ... YOU ... dooo-ING?" He calls my mom and sister in, "Listen to this," he told them: "WHAT .... ARE ... YOU ...doING?"

Collectively, we were simply amazed... that really was Dad's voice!

Well, at least some version of his voice.

I got ready to grab the recorder and head off to my room to have some fun with my new gift. Dad stopped me and said, "Give me that tape, I want to save that."

I was confused. Save that? It wasn't even anything... just some pseudo-robot asking one question. Despite my hesitation, I turned it over. After all, I did get the two-pack of tapes.

Over the next few days, Dad kept borrowing the recorder whenever one of his friends would call. I would hear him tell them, "You've got to hear this." Then he'd turn on the recorder, and I'd hear robot man asking, "WHAT .... ARE ... YOU ... dooo-ING?" This was followed by laughter and him swearing that was actually a recording, and it was him. He could prove it by replaying it again, which he would then do.

Seriously, who were these guys who thought this was good entertainment?

A month or so later, Dad walked by my room, and I had all of my Batman action figures out and was staging a Batman fight. I was recording, complete with me singing the Batman theme and punctuating it with the occasional "POW," "BAM" or "ZAP" like they did in those campy fights on the show. When he asked what I was doing, I told him I was taping a Batman fight.

"These tapes are expensive" he told me, "you can't simply waste them." Since I was confused on how a Batman fight wasn't as important as robot man, combined with the fact I didn't need it to record minutes from any business meetings at age 10, I never used the tape recorder again.

Even though this wasn't a "great holiday memory," it certainly stands out. Every once in a while, I'll come across that tape, find an old boom box, and play robot man for a good laugh.

Chapter Ten: The Letter

I'll admit, I like "reality TV." *Survivor, Big Brother, The Biggest Loser...* all good stuff. I was actually an early adopter of this genre. As a kid I loved the shows *That's Incredible* and *Real People*. Looking back now, I think we realize how lame these shows really were, but in their day, they were big.

One of the coolest components of *Real People* was the fact that if you contributed to the show, they actually sent you a REAL PEOPLE T-SHIRT! All the kids in my class wanted one of those shirts. If I could only get one of those shirts, I knew I'd have a happy life from that moment forward. I could be the coolest kid in the school. I just had to figure out how to score one.

I told my Dad about how great it would be to land an official *Real People* t-shirt, and he was intrigued. I could see the "wheels churning" as I explained all you had to do was contribute something like a wacky classified ad, funny newspaper headline or misprinted flier. He took all of this in and said, "We'll find something for you to get on that show."

In the meantime, other kids in my class were sending things in, hoping to score a shirt of their own. About a month or so later, my Dad presents me with a newspaper article which showed a mix-up on a local street sign at a busy intersection. You go one way, it's Olive Street Road. You go the other way it's Olive Street Road... which way do you go? Who knows!!! Ah, nutty 80's hilarity at its best!

The actual photo/story wasn't bad. Perhaps it was even *Real People* material. My enthusiasm was short lived though. A swift kick in the jacobs was about to take place. In my Dad's other hand, he had a hand written page.

"Here you go, Steve, I even wrote out what you need to say to be sure to get on the show," he instructed me. Below is basically what was written on the piece of paper:

Dear Real People,
I found this article in our local newspaper. It seems we've had a mix-up here in St. Louis. I'm worried Santa may be confused by the street signs. Could you please notify him and let him know where my house is so he doesn't get lost. I want to be sure to get my toys this year.
Sincerely,
Steve Akley
P.S. – My little sister is worried, too. Can you please tell Santa not to forget her. Also, she's a fan of the show. Can you send a t-shirt for her as well?

Great stuff… if you're FOUR years old I think.

"Dad, I'm 12 years old. I can't send this. The kids at school would beat me up if it got on the air. I haven't believed in Santa for like 8 years. Plus, who cares about Kelly getting a shirt. I don't want to be a nerd, wearing the same shirt as my sister."

The old man is FURIOUS. "Not only will you submit this," he tells me, "you're going to turn it in with the letter I wrote for you; and you're going to write it perfectly. They like cute, and they like neat."

Perfectly?

Okay, I got my out now. I'll just screw up his "Dear Santa" crap a couple of times and I'm off the hook. With him over my shoulder, I start the letter, "Dear Real *Peple*."

"GOD DAMMIT," (as only he can say), as he grabs my letter tears it up and throws it away. "Start again. This is for national TV."

About two lines in, another screw up. Once again, he tears it up. Third time… third f'up.

This time he's livid. He takes his ample belt off and lays it next to me. "You screw it up again, you're getting it."

Now he's yelling at me. I'm crying like the four year old who should be writing this sappy ass shit, and the old man is threatening me with bodily harm if I make another mistake in this ridiculous letter. I thought this was going to be a fun project about me. At this point, I'm not even sure who wants this shirt… me or him. As I begin to write again, actually trying this time mind you, I screw it up on the last line. I beg him to just let me make one little "cross-through" and complete the letter. Nope. Trash can and start again.

Finally I get through a perfect version on the fifth try. Thankfully, I was spared my dignity as that pile of sappy crap never made it on the air. That's as close as I ever was, or ever want to be, to participating in reality TV myself!

Chapter Eleven: The Bowtie

For reasons unbeknownst to me, there are people out there who continue to tell jokes. I can't say I have NEVER laughed at a joke, but overall, I believe that the joke is the single most overrated form of entertainment. It gets quite uncomfortable for me when you get the person who thinks that they are a "joke teller."

Now here's a person who wants to be funny, but his or her only way to go about doing it is recycle the same overtold dumbass jokes that have been around forever. Of course, you, as the "listener," are forced to politely laugh at these morons so as to not hurt the "jokesters" feelings.

Let me tell you something: the stuff that happens to you in everyday living is way funnier than anything that starts out like, "Two blondes walk into a bar…" The great thing about real life, it's true, thereby at least doubling the impact of anything remotely funny.

Unfortunately, my dad was always a bit of a jokester. I have to admit, I shuddered every time someone said to me, "Boy, your dad is funny; he's got a lot of great jokes." He wasn't one of the "serial offenders" I was talking about above, but he did tell quite a few jokes.

WHY? I don't know. He always had more funny things happen to him than practically anyone I know. The good thing about real life anecdotes is the fact you can enjoy them again and again.

Take, for instance, this little gem from when my sister got married…

Always a hectic time, my sister's wedding was just like everyone else's. Everybody wants the "perfect wedding," and nobody wants to be the person who messes it up, so there is always that underlying pressure surrounding a wedding. We get to the wedding date, and my mom and sister leave my dad alone to get ready as they are out getting her hair done. Based on the fact my mom cared for him as if he was an invalid, my dad had the independence skills of your average three-year-old, so he's already got quite a bit working against him.

As he goes to get dressed, he's feeling the underlying pressure of just not wanting to screw this wedding up. All he wants to do is his part and get through the day. As he opens the closet door, "Shit, no tuxedo!"

Unbelievably, my future brother-in-law, the "groom to-be," who had been staying with my parents, must have grabbed it as he left. (He spent the night before the wedding at a hotel with his family.) Well, now Larry is in a full panic. No tuxedo and no real way to get ahold of Jeff. He's totally f'ed he thinks. He calls the hotel. No Jeff Brooks registered. He tells the clerk it's an emergency and he begins calling room-to-room, to the wedding guests staying there. Finally he gets Jeff's mother on the phone. He relays the whole story of Jeff taking dad's tuxedo, how he has to get it back, etc. She tracks down Jeff and tells the story to him.

One problem... Jeff doesn't have the tuxedo.

FINALLY, after all of that, my dad suddenly remembers he had thought ahead that he and Jeff having a tuxedo in the same closet might have cause a problem, so he put it in a different closet. While quite embarrassing, he's just relieved he's actually got the damn tuxedo.

Ah, another funny story the family will be reliving again-and-again, right?

Wait, there's more…

SIDE NOTE: You know how you've got that "little man in your head?" You know that person, known as your conscious, who directs you within the walls of your skull. Well, Larry didn't have that (apparently, his little man was my mom), so he had no one to tell him, "hmmmm tuxedo gone…I moved a tuxedo earlier in week."

But I digress…

So now he's having a really bad day. Running a little late because of the delay in finding the tuxedo. Embarrassed about how it came up missing. His "little man" off somewhere on a hairdresser adventure, he's flustered. He now must dress quickly and get to the church.

He gets the tux on and is ready to go. One last accessory to put on and he's out the door… the bowtie.

He takes the tie out of the bag, and thinks it looks a little small. He takes the "pre-tied" bowtie and goes to slide it over his head.

As hard as it is to believe, that tie gets stuck, right above his eyebrows. Won't go up. Won't go down. Just a perfectly placed propeller, right in the middle of his forehead.

What you would do here is irrelevant. You have the benefit of a little man weighing your options for you. Larry didn't have that benefit. Plus, his only goal was to not trash the wedding, so now here he stands with a bowtie over his head not knowing what to do.

Thought's race through his head:

"Get this stupid tie off."

"Don't be late."

"I've already been humiliated with the earlier 'lost tuxedo' incident."

"I don't want to f'up the wedding."

"I think I actually like the Ranch Doritos better than the Nacho ones."

After one last tug to determine it wouldn't budge (believe me, I still have no idea how you can get a tie where it won't go up or down), he did the only thing anybody would do, he cut the tie off, put it on and pinned the strap underneath the collar.

Okay, I made that up.

That's what anyone else would have done. Instead, Larry, aka "propeller boy," gets in the car and drives to the tuxedo place. As he pulls in, he looks over at the car next to him, and in just his latest bit of bad luck, there sits a couple, staring face-to-face with a man with a bow tie in the middle of his forehead.

He storms into the shop, which, of course, is packed with people. Apparently, feeling he was having a tuxedo "emergency," he walked right past everyone in line and went straight to the front. Screw protocol, this is a sixty-year-old man with an f'ing bowtie in the middle of his forehead.

While much of this story left me wondering how this happened, on this point the Akester and I were in complete agreement: you get cart blanche ability to jump to the front of the line if you've got the stones to walk into a crowded store looking like that.

By this point in the story, I'm always about ready to piss in my pants, so I've never got him to tell me if the clerk said, "May I help you" as he came to the front of the line, or if she had the diagnostic skills to instantly recognize his problem on her own. I do know that one thing the clerk did say was the funniest goddamn thing about the whole story. This teenage clerk had the ability (apparently, she does have a little man in her head) to figure out how embarrassing the situation was, so she told my dad, "Oh, this happens all the time. In fact, we've had to cut them off of their foreheads before."

Here's a guy, who is a retired police Major, who believes that line of bull crap. Oddly, he is comforted by the fact that others have shared in this same experience.

YEAH RIGHT!

I can see every Saturday morning two or three guys walking through the door, having unsuccessfully attempted to slide a bowtie over their heads, having not had the wits about them to actually open the strap and fasten it around their necks.

The funny thing is, I'm convinced that's the only reason we've gotten to hear the story. He believed the future "employee of the month's" story so much that his comfort led him to sharing it with me, and ultimately you. Thank you eighteen-year old store clerk!!!!!

By the way, forget the jokes, I told you real life is funny enough!

Chapter Twelve: The Steps

Do you believe that your subconscious can actually control your body and actions?

Well, I do and I'd like to present a clear-cut case to you which I think clearly shows the subconscious can actually control the mind and body.

When I was a kid, my mom started bowling in a weekday afternoon league. Who do you think has their afternoons free during the week?

Working women? Of course not. They are busy at their jobs.

Stay-at-home mothers? Hell no. They've got kids to look after.

The answer: old broads!

That's right, my mom, and three friends, joined a league of blue-haired, confused grannies. This went on from the time I was five until well after I was out of the house. You'd think she'd be ready for the pro circuit, but her average remained in the 130's when she hung it up after 30+ years on the lanes.

Anyway, when you're in your 20's and everyone else is in their 70's (back when she started), you're pretty damn good. Your "buck, twenty-nine" score looks like a PBA hall-of-famer when your rolling against a gal named Helga who's 78 years old and just got her high game of the year with a 56.

Pretty soon, they are dominating the league. Trophies are rolling in. My mom accumulates them on a shelf going down the steps to the basement. (Nothing really acknowledges your redneck roots like a shelf full of bowling trophies, does it?) While my dad never said a word about them, looking back, I'm thinking they got to him.

Think about it. Here's a woman, a housewife, who is bringing home a trophy every year showcasing her as the best of her sport. She was an athlete, at the top of her game.

What was my Dad?

He didn't have any athletic trophies. He wasn't in any leagues. I bet every time he opened up the door to the basement they mocked him. Large-boobed, flowing haired, female keglers on top of all of those trophies, all nice and neat in a row.

"Larry……Larry……Larry," they would beckon to him, "1st Place 1975, 1st Place 1976, 1st Place 1977…" as he'd mutter to himself, "I'm not a loser, I'm not a loser, I'm not a loser…"

As the last trophy was put in place in the mid-80's (looks like we were going to have to add a new shelf), something must have taken over inside of Larry. His subconscious must have finally decided to take action. One day as he was getting ready for work, he headed for the stairs as he always did… dress shirt, black socks (I mean really hideous dress socks. He owned two styles of socks: both the ultra thin/almost nylons material… the ones that go just to the ankle, have elastic at the top, but are real loose-fitting everywhere else and the ones that went way over the calf, to the bend in the knee. Either way, it's a pretty ugly picture.) and a pair of his patent leather work shoes. So here he was: police shirt, a pair of full-cut, big-boy sized Fruit of the Looms, fugly dress socks and his patent leather police issue uniform shoes.

What's missing?

His pants. For reasons only known to Larry, when dressing, it was always drawers, shirt, socks, shoes, and finally, pants. The pants were always last thing before heading out the door. That was always enough motivation to keep you sleeping in until after he had left.

So, he's got everything on but the pants. They are downstairs (where they get ironed). He heads down the steps in his unique outfit (everyone else in the house still in bed). Next thing you know, we hear pure chaos.

Uh oh, Larry's falling down the steps. He's always been an animated "faller" but this was Academy Award stuff, even for him. I didn't see it, but it must have been quite a show. Arms flailing.. feet flying, fun.

In the meantime, he's screaming the shit he's taking out as he goes. Almost like a play-by-play announcer.

I kid you not, the fall "sounded" like this:

"AHHHHHHH... ...CRASH.... ....OH NO, THE BANNISTER... RIP... .. CRASH ... .BOOM... THE TROPHIES ..... AHHHHHHHHHHHHH ....SMACK BOOM...."

Sure enough, he smashed up a bunch of the trophies, along with some miscellaneous other crap.

About a week later, same scenario (no pants, police shoes/black safety socks), "AHHHHHH ….CRASH ….. THE TROPHIES …. BOOM …. SMASH …. OH, THE PICTURES …. CRASH ….. BOOM ….. BANG…."

Son of a bitch, he did it again! More of the trophies were trashed. (Well, the problem of finding more room for them is now officially been resolved.)

If the story ended here, it could be written off as a coincidence, but it doesn't end here.

About a month and a half later, Larry, aka Underwear Walker did it again, "AHHHHHHHHH ….. CRASH ….. THE TROPHIES … BOOM … .AHHHHHHHH …… BANG ….. THE PHOTO FRAMES … BOOM… SHIT, I'VE GOT A SMALL WANG … CRASH……."

Okay, okay, you've got me. I made up the yelling about the small wang, but goddamn you gotta admit that was kinda funny. All right, back to the story…

That's right, the rest of the trophies…toast. I'm not shitting you. Two months, three falls, complete devastation to trophyville. That little shelf was Tokyo to Larry's Godzilla act.

The subconscious is a dangerous place.

Respect it or you'll pay. If you don't believe that Larry's actions were the result of his subconscious taking over, consider this: he fell three times in two months, not having fallen down those steps in the 15 years or so before in that house, and he didn't fall down them again after all the trophies were gone.

Chapter Thirteen: The A++++

In college I once had a professor who would spend as much time bragging about his handball skills as he did on the coursework. He had a standing offer with the class… if you could beat him in a set, you get an A. He always stated he set forth this same challenge in his 20+ years of teaching, and he'd never been beaten by a student.

In college, I played a little Wiffle ball, possessed a decent game of foosball, and experienced my share of victories in couch wrestling, but I wasn't a handball player. One of my dad's co-workers, a fellow policeman, did play a lot, though, so I hatched a scheme and approached my professor.

What if I didn't play, but I could set up a match with a fellow handball player? Would the offer of an A still be on the table?

My professor agreed to this unique challenge so I set up the match. I didn't realize it at the time, but in the gym wasn't the only type of handball my "happily married" professor liked to play. My dad brought his buddy to the match, a fellow policeman, and this officer quickly realized he had recently arrested the professor in St. Louis' Forest Park in a car in the middle of a sexual encounter with another man. That made for an awkward "how do you do," that's for sure.

Nothing was stated at the match… in fact, I didn't find out about that nugget until a few weeks later. While it was obvious the professor was shaken, I didn't know about the "back" story, and he sure as hell wasn't going to bring it up… neither was my dad's buddy, so they just played. They were to play the best of three but it was all over after my dad's friend won 21-0 in the first two games of the set.

Who knows if he had made up the skills he claimed to posses, been so flustered about the awkwardness of the encounter or just went easy on my dad's buddy in hopes of him not saying anything to me. Either way, I sailed through the rest of that class without ever opening the book again!

Chapter Fourteen: The Dash

When my sister was between the ages of 3 and 4, she went through a phase where she would throw-up every time we went out to eat. I am not sure what causes an affliction like this. Without fail though, if we were out to eat, at some point during the dinner she would pipe in, "Mommy, I am going to be sick."

If you ever find yourself with a child that suffers from this "disease … phobia … psychosis … whatever," you will quickly learn to take heed when the kid says he or she is sick.

The first couple of times were the worst. My mom would start questioning her about it, and then she just starts chuckin' right there at the table. We had a real bad incident at Denny's. She went all "Exorcist" right as the meal was served, and you've got vomit all over the food, on the tables, rolling off of the edge onto the floor. The only saving grace was the fact it was Denny's. I got the feeling it happens about 2 or 3 times a week there.

After that incident, as soon as she said she was sick, my mom would grab her and just start running to the bathroom. Her success rate was solid, so we could begin to enjoy dinners out again. The funny thing was, as soon as we'd leave the restaurant she was fine, so it wasn't like she was really sick.

This one night, we had the chance to go with a group to Shakey's Pizza. I loved that place. The best part was you could actually watch the chefs making the pizza there.

They're in a glass enclosed kitchen where you could watch them tossing the dough up in the air.

My mom was a little worried about taking "vomit girl" out with friends, but she hoped that maybe with a group she wouldn't get sick. Unfortunately, about ¾ of the way through the meal, we hear, "Mom, I'm going to be sick." Chaos ensues as my mom dashes to try to grab her. As my dad tries to jump up to help out, he loses control of his stool.

No, you dumbass…. he didn't shit his pants; they had bar stools for chairs. He fell straight back off of the stool and landed in a perfect seated position on that stool, flat on his back (feet crooked up hugging the stool and straight out).

The whole restaurant now stops.

Conversations cease.

Waitresses look over.

Chefs drop their pizza crusts.

 The whole place just shut down and became silent as they looked on to see what in the hell happened.

Slowly…..deliberately….an arm rose from the fallen comrade. Like ET, the index finger extends up in the air and Larry says, "Take her to the bathroom!"

Everything turned out fine as my mom made it with her to the restroom. My dad, along with everyone else, had a great laugh about this at the restaurant. Of course, once the friends are gone, and we get to the car, we found out how pissed he was about the fall. He threatened to kill my sister if she ever threw-up in a restaurant again. I guess she was scared straight because she's now has a streak of not throwing up in restaurants dating all the way back to 1974!

Chapter Fifteen: The Stories

Growing up in my house, there was one common bond. It wasn't religion, love of sports, or time spent at the dinner table like most families. Ours was simply the fart. My parents both loved flatulence. Now I'm of the belief that if you can set aside the science whereby flatulence is simply gases created from decaying food, which have been expelled from one person's body via the cornshoot; that in-turn have now entered your olfactory system via your nasal passage, I would agree there is some humor tied to farting. It just shouldn't be something which just automatically causes the biggest belly laugh possible anytime someone even mentions the word.

That's basically how my parents were though. If someone farted in a movie, it didn't matter what happened for the rest of the 90-minutes of the film, it was a great movie. There would be times when they would sit around in the living room, or perhaps in bed, and they would just rehash the fart incidents in their life.

I would literally hear the same stories, over-and-over. The best part is in any of the stories that involve them "dealing", they are portrayed as deftly dropping a bomb and swiftly moving away, leaving plausible deniability lest anyone perhaps think they are the offenders. They takes turns telling the stories that are literally like, "Remember, when we were at the dime store," my dad would start, "You were in the checkout line. I dropped that stink bomb and left. You had to stay there to pay. (note: both parents are nearly in tears by this point from laughter.) That cashier had no idea what happened there."

Somebody tell me why dropping ass in front of a cashier is funny? How is it they think that the cashier doesn't know it was the Akester who crapped his pants when there is a nostril-stinging, sulfur smell and a large yeti-like man running from the area, laughing like a hyena, so he can get to a safe point to watch what is going on? Boy, she has no idea it was him who soiled himself. I'll bet she was wondering if she did it herself.

Yeah right. It's called a society. People are polite. Yes, they aren't calling out the shit-smelling, running yeti-man, but trust me, she knew.

At some point, the conversation always had to turn to people who farted in front of them. The funny thing is, in their stories, these people are never individuals who should be lauded for their hilarious hijinks. These are individuals who should be cast from society for that lack of social decorum.

Moving on from my dad's dime store story, he very well may have transitioned to another of his favorites, "You remember that son-of-a-bitch who was stocking that Pepsi in the grocery store? I don't know who the hell he thinks he is…that was just rotten. That som' bitch ought to be shot for dropping a stench like that in public."

This is no less confusing to me today as it was in the 1970's. Why in the hell is Larry damn near a national hero in his story of silent but deadly, but the Pepsi stock guy is nothing but a lowlife piece of garbage? The funny thing was, my dad had the mother of embarrassing public gas expulsion stories. He just didn't like to tell that particular story.

The crown jewel of his embarrassing flatulence stories occurred in the swinging 70s when my parents went out to dinner with another couple. This was a fancy steakhouse with a salad bar. While common place now, and perhaps even pushed down the food chain to lower-end restaurants, at the time, this was only something you'd find at a high end eatery. No one else elected to add the salad bar, but my dad thought it would be a nice accoutrement to his meal.

He heads off to salad-a-paloozza. My dad jumps in a line and plans on tearing this salad bar up!

As he is standing there, a sudden sneeze comes on and flies out. What he didn't realize is he had an air bomb in the cylinder ready to be fired as well. The force of that unexpected sneeze caused him to relax the hold button for just a nano-second, and it was *"RELEASE THE HOUNDS"* time! Yes, it's true, in conjunction with that sneeze, Larry ripped a heinous, loud, echoing show stopper, "Brrrrfflllllhhhhhpppp."

The guy behind him in line lets out a yell, "WHOA!"

There was no ambiguity here. Half of the people in the restaurant were in line for the salad haberdashery, and they had just been hit with cruise missile. The Akester immediately starts to turn to shag ass out of there. The stench already begins to take effect on those poor bastards in line. There were a few "ughs," some hand waving, and even a nostrils pinch witnessed by Larry as he hustled out of there and back to the table.

Of course, his co-diners start grilling him why he didn't get any salad. He tries not to tell them, but it was just too good not to share. They spent the rest of the dinner laughing uncontrollably, trying to figure out who was giving them dirty stares because they were being loud and who was giving them dirty stares because a member of their table had dropped a "hot sauerkraut shot" on them.

Chapter Sixteen: The Encounter

June 22, 1983.

It was a date in history that changed my life dramatically and still haunts me to this day.

Okay, I admit that is an overstatement. I do think about that day an awful lot though. I had just completed my freshman year of high school and was at that weird age of "you think you know everything but you really can't do anything since you aren't yet old enough to have a regular job or drive a car." To break up the summer monotony of street baseball and swimming, my dad offered to take me with him to work one day.

At the time, my dad was a St. Louis policeman. Now you're probably thinking for a 15-year old guy that sounds pretty exciting. Well, you'd be wrong. My dad was known for his prowess in writing and administrative duties more than "capturing perps," so his job was more administrative than police work. Kind of like an office job with a badge ("You know these personnel policies don't write themselves," he'd tell me.)

The real hook to get me to go was a planned stop by Rawlings, the sporting goods manufacturer. They manufactured and sewed right on the spot and any irregulars were thrown in these big bins on pallets. Depending on what bin you were foraging through (truly foraging mind you, there was no organization to these things... that was actually part of the allure) your cost was either 50 cents or a buck. Some of the stuff they'd even give you for free. This wasn't junk...quality stuff for sports teams around the country and sometimes you couldn't even tell what was wrong (I was destined to be the best dressed street baseballer in the area).

When my dad and I arrived we were instructed to sit in the waiting room. This wasn't something they did for the public; you had to be a policeman and there was a guy who had to escort since you would be on the floor of a working manufacturing facility. We took our seats in the small reception area. We began to have small chat about afternoon plans:

Dad: Steve, I know you've been bored with the day thus far, but I've got some good police type of things for us to do this afternoon you might be interested in.

Steve: Oh yeah, Dad, what's that?

Dad: We're going to review the officer's manual in the area of rest breaks. Our officers are allocated two 15-minute breaks for an 8-hour shift. If they are forced to work overtime, there isn't a stipulation in there about further breaks... I'm strongly considering adding a third break for such situations. You see, when you empower your officers with the tools to be successful, you have a productive police force. Now that's police work!

Little did I know my rescue from the compelling "officer's break routine" conversation was about to walk right through the door. As we sat there, awaiting our turn to comb through boxes of three-legged shorts and shirts with no neck holes to find some gems, in walked Bob Uecker.

Of course at that time, for sports fans like dad and me, there probably wasn't a better known TV pitchman in the world of sports. He was on the Miller Lite commercials with those great self-deprecating moments where he was always assuming he was "going to be in the front row" with some free tickets, and he'd end up in the last row of the stadium. He strolled up to the receptionist and didn't say anything (I'm guessing he thought she would recognize him). What unfolded next seemed like something out of one of his commercials (today, you would have to assume you were on some kind of undercover stunt if this played out right in front of you):

Receptionist: Yes sir, can I help you.

Uecker: I'm here to see Ted Hansen.

Receptionist: Well what's your name sir?

Uecker: Bob Uecker.

Receptionist (confused): Again?

Uecker: Bob Uecker.

Receptionist (ringing Mr. Hansen): Yes, I have a Bob..Yuck,,,Yeck...excuse me, what was that name again sir?

Uecker: Bob Uecker.

Receptionist: Yes, Mr. Hansen, I have a Bob Ucker here to see you. (Note: she still got it wrong with the "uck" sound instead of the correct "euch".)

She then hung up the phone and told Bob Uecker that Mr. Hansen was busy, and he was going to have to have a seat in the waiting room.

So there dad and I are, two huge sports fans, sitting next to Bob Uecker. We're whispering back-and-forth, laughing at what we had just witnessed. Uecker seemed kind of befuddled by the whole thing, but I could tell he knew we recognized him.

The funny thing was that my dad even had a natural in to break the ice in a conversation since he had pulled Uecker over back when he played with the Cardinals. Alas, we didn't talk to him. Living in St. Louis, you don't run into random celebrities, and I don't know if it was we didn't know what to say, or we just wanted to leave the guy alone (who knows, he may have had some great insight for dad on that break policy). Either way, we didn't get anything signed, much less have any sort of conversation.

I still kick myself about not saying anything to Uecker to this day. Not because I didn't get an autograph, or even to hear some of the funny stuff he talks about on TV. It just seems like it would have been a great opportunity to sit down with a very likeable guy, in a casual setting, who has been in baseball his whole life and to simply talk to him about the game. Now that would have been cool!

Oh well, I can always say I "sat in the front row" with Bob Uecker, even if it was just in a company's waiting room.

Chapter Seventeen: The Roll

The second week of June in 1985 was going to be the ultimate Akley family week. My dad, who never took a week of vacation at a time, decided to take a whole week of vacation (unheard of) …and he said he wouldn't call in to the office all week (outrageous). My dad lived for his job. He'd leave for work at 6:00 a.m., and get home about 7:00 at night. On weekends, he'd work secondary. The whole time he'd be telling us how great his job was. Looking back, his being gone so much probably allowed us to keep our sanity, but I can say as it was happening, not everyone in the family was real pleased about it.

Since he was going to be off all week, I took the week off from work as well. My mom planned some cool things to do around town, and we were going to enjoy some dinners out… in between everything, we'd just hang out at the house as a family and swim.

The first day of vacation we were in the pool, and my dad was in a particularly reflective mood. Talking about how relaxing it was. How much he was looking forward to just hanging out with the family. We go to get out of the pool, and my dad is the last one out. It was an above ground pool, so you climb out and onto a deck, and then head down a ladder to the yard.

As my dad hits the last step on the way down to the yard, we hear the sound of wood cracking. I've never heard a redwood drop, but this is clearly what it would sound like.

Akester starts yelling "Whooooooa" and the final noise was him hitting a large stepping stone we had at the base of the ladder which held the foot bath. (The little tub of water you stepped in to clean any dirt or grass off of your feet before getting in the pool.) I would say the sound of him hitting the stepping stone could best be described as dropping a garbage bag full of skin from a 2-story building.

Akester hits the ground and just starts rolling. I mean he's like one of those douche bags you see on TV who chase a big giant wheel of cheese down that steep hill in England and invariably trip and start rolling about halfway down. The whole time he's rolling he's emitting a series of groans… kinda like, "ahhh … ahhhhhhh … ahhhh … ahhhh….ahhh!"

I'll be honest, I didn't even know what the hell was going on at that moment. We've got wood cracking and bags of skin dropping noises. There's this 300 lb. guy, who's just had some sort of bodily trauma, screaming like an injured chimp, and he's taken off rolling towards the neighbor's house.

My mom is going, "Larry, what are you doing?" He makes it all the way to the fence at the edge of the yard and then he just starts thrashing back-and-forth.

My mom is continuing to try to talk to him but he's still just screaming and thrashing. Years later he would tell us he was trying to "roll off" the pain. We often would wonder if we didn't have the fence if he could have successfully rolled off such a heinous injury. I'm thinking by the time he rolled to Telegraph Road (about a mile away), he would have been fine.

As all of this rolling, thrashing, screaming and moaning is going on, I can't help but think, "Come on, it was like a 6-inch freefall here. How bad can it be?"

As these thoughts race through my head, I just get to laughing at this whole scene. I step behind a beach towel hanging on a clothesline in the backyard, laugh hysterically, and take a moment to absorb what I just witnessed. I compose myself and come out from behind the towel.

By this time he's stopped rolling around. His ankles are blown up like beach balls and he keeps saying "my wrist, my wrist" as he's moves the wrist around in a circle. (Yeah, maybe if you would quit twisting the f'ing thing it wouldn't hurt so much.) My mom instructs me to call an ambulance. "No," my dad interjects. "I'll be okay. Just give me a minute."

We finally help him get up. He uses my mom like a crutch, putting his weight on her to get to the car. We go to the hospital. The diagnosis: two sprained ankles and a sprained wrist. The old man isn't worried about screwing up the vacation, or really about the injuries, as much as he is concerned about work. His only question for the doctor was, will he be able to go back to work on a week from Monday. That's when his vacation would end and he'd have to take a sick day. He had worked for the police department for 25 years by that point and never taken a sick day. The doctor wouldn't commit to anything, but he didn't think it looked good to get back to work by Monday.

We get back home, which by this point is a few hours later. After we get dad in bed to rest, my mom's back starts to lock up. She has injured it helping my dad to the car. His weight on her threw her back out. Now we had two people laid up in bed.

The rest of the ultimate Akley family week, in the summer of '85, was spent waiting hand-and-foot on two gimped up fools. They had a bell which they would ring any time they need my sister or me to get them some food, help them to the restroom, watch my dad twist his wrist stating, "uhhhh, it's my wrist," (again, quit twisting it and maybe it would be okay) or get them more food.

A week from that Monday, my dad put on his police uniform and headed off to work. His prized attendance record would remain intact. I'm sure he was telling all of his buddies about his injuries and how he "toughed it out" afterwards. I'm guessing his story didn't include the screaming, moaning, rolling and thrashing back-and-forth!

Chapter Eighteen: The Sandwich

My dad was never much of a cook.

Believe it or not, that may be the understatement of all understatements. Despite my father's large appetite, he didn't cook anything for himself. You'd think a guy of his size would be all over food, any way, anyhow. While his ability to consume may have be unparalleled, he didn't cook. Literally, if my mom was somewhere else, he'd be sitting around waiting for her to get home to prepare his lunch. That doesn't mean he wouldn't mow through a bag of chips or eat a meter or chocolate; he just would not prepare anything.

There was only one exception to this during my childhood growing up in that house. When I was about 13 years old, my mom was out somewhere around lunch time. My dad suggested we make some sandwiches. He goes to the refrigerator and pulls out the bologna. I take one look at it and notice a thick coating of slime on the lunch meat he has just grabbed. Being a typical 13-year-old a'hole, I don't say anything, other than politely declining the sandwich offer as I sit back to watch this thing play out.

Sure enough, he goes ahead and makes the sandwich and takes a bite. I can smell the goddamn thing from across the room. Nothing from him though, he takes another bite. About halfway through the sandwich, my mom gets home. She sees that dad is eating that bologna that has been open in the fridge for God knows how long and starts yelling at him. "Larry, what in the hell are you doing? You idiot. It has green slime in the package," as she holds up a piece to demonstrate gooey slime slowly cascading down a wretched smelling piece of bologna.

Despite the fact my dad doesn't think it's a big deal, he heads to toss the last two bites of the sandwich in the trash. I finally interject and ask him why he doesn't finish it. If the taste didn't bother him, surely those last two bites aren't going to do any more damage than already has been done. Alas, he wouldn't budge. The rest of the sandwich hit the trash can and he never "cooked" again!

Chapter Nineteen: The Bathroom

One summer, my mom, dad, Amy, Cat and I headed to Pensacola, Fla. for a vacation. For the most part it went remarkably well. We had some fun at the beach and enjoyed some great restaurants.

It was at one of those restaurants we had a "book worthy" incident, though. After going to the restroom upon arrival, I noticed that above the "Men's Room" sign there was an arrow which stated, "over there" pointing to the other restroom with a similar sign. I guess it was sort of a cheeky joke to get you confused as to which restroom to go in. I noticed when you went in the bathroom, there was a huge sign which read "THIS IS THE MEN'S ROOM" and I'm guessing there was a similar one in the ladies room in case you mistakenly went in the wrong one based upon the misleading signage on the door.

I honestly didn't think a whole lot about the situation as it happened. It wasn't until the Akester said he needed to stop by the bathroom before we left. I told him where the restroom was but his eyes glazed over as I tried to explain how to get there in this large establishment.

I thought, what the hell, I'll take him there; then I can see him read the wrong sign and start to head into the wrong restroom. We get there, sure enough, he goes to the bathroom marked, "Men's (over there)" and headed in. He ignored the foot high letters saying it was actually the ladies room and went in.

I would find out later, he thought it was an odd "Florida thing" that they didn't have urinals but just proceeded to a stall. I'm outside the bathroom dying laughing. He's been in there quite awhile; then a woman walks right by me into the restroom. I can actually hear the conversation through the door.

Dad: Excuse me ma'am, you are in the men's room. The ladies room is next door.

Lady: No, this is the ladies room.

Dad: No it isn't.

Lady: They have confusing signs on the door, this is the ladies room. See, there are no urinals.

Dad: AHHHHHHHHHHH (Note: He emitted a very high pitched scream… hey, he actually screamed like a chick, maybe he did belong there).

He literally comes running out of the bathroom, I'm just about on the floor laughing, and I go to say something to him and he just rushes by me into the men's room stating, "YOU COCKSUCKER!"

I'm not exactly sure what I did here. I didn't suggest a restroom for him to go into. I didn't open the ladies room door for him. I was every bit the victim here as him, right?

I really do not know what he is doing at this point. I mean I know he went to the bathroom already because I heard him flush and then wash his hands where he got into the debate with the woman in the ladies room. Now he's back in the bathroom?

Did he just happen to need to go again?

Did the embarrassment of the ladies room exchange bring on a spontaneous bout of diarrhea?

Did he assume he committed a crime so he was officially on the lam?

Five minutes go by… no Akester. Ten. Still in the restroom.

Finally, 20 minutes later he emerges and says, "Let's go." He was hot as a firecracker at me so we didn't even discuss it. We basically ignored the situation and just spent the rest of the time going to the beach and restaurants with well-marked restrooms.

Chapter Twenty: The Singer

While my dad may have been the root cause for many of the stories in this book, this one is a little different. He really didn't do anything wrong, but as usual he's at the center of the story. We were in Branson enjoying some family time with Amy, Cat and I along with my mom and dad. We went to breakfast at this little diner right across from our hotel.

It's Branson "hokey" with a man and woman belting out country tunes live while you eat breakfast. We avoid this whole "show aspect" of the breakfast by sitting on the opposite side of the restaurant. The waitress we had was a little spacey. She even saw my dad taking his morning medication and joked she wouldn't mind having a few of those pills.

Another group comes over to our section and an outspoken member of their group states he's not doing bad for a guy having a birthday. He sits down at the table right next to us, in the same spot where my dad was seated at our table. A little later, the waitress comes over and asks Cat what my dad's name is.

She doesn't think anything about it and tells her it's Lawrence. We didn't know what was going on so we just continued to go about eating our breakfast.

Then we hear the singer (not in view of us where we have positioned ourselves) tell the audience we have a "birthday boy" here. Our waitress comes over and tells my dad, "Hey "birthday boy you have to go up to the stage!" There's much commotion going on so he didn't get the chance to tell her it's not his birthday and he's not going to the stage. Then we hear the singer approaching us. "Where's Lawrence," he says. No need to head up to the stage, he's got a wireless mic.

My dad's trying to say it's not his birthday, but the guy starts singing. He gets to the "Happy Birthday, Dear Lawrence," portion of the song...and he pauses and says, "To You, and ONLY YOU LAWRENCE... that's called cruise ship style," and then he finishes out the song.

I was mortified because I thought at any second my dad was going to grab that wireless microphone and go into the whole story about how he sat down, was eating, how much he likes the breakfast ham there, how this other birthday guy came in and sat at the same seat at a different table and everything just confused. Thankfully, he didn't do any of that. By the end of the song, he was waving his arms over his head, basking in the cruise ship-style birthday wishes the restaurant was bestowing on him.

While we always celebrated his real birthday on August 20th, from that point forward we also acknowledged his "Branson Birthday" every May 1st.

Chapter Twenty-One: The Chapstick

The Chapstick story was destined to be one of a classic from the moment it happened. On December 4th, just 8 days before he died, as we were leaving a Subway restaurant, Akester overheard a conversation my mom and I were having and he jumped in.

The only problem was he hadn't heard correctly what we were talking about so what followed was typical Akester chaos.

Sandy: I really like this chocolate mint flavored Chapstick.

Steve: That may actually be a flavor I would try. I like Burt's Bees and it too is mint.

Sandy: So you like the idea of chocolate and mint huh?

Larry: I ate those mints.

Sandy: You ate a Chapstick?

Larry: It's chocolate and mint.

Sandy: So you ate it?

Larry: It was from Cat. That stuff she was just selling.

Sandy: The boys actually just sold stuff. There was Chapstick in there?

Larry: Yeah, I ate it.

Sandy: You ate Chapstick?

Larry: It's chocolate and mint.

Sandy: Okay, but why would you eat it?

Larry (anger rising): IT'S CHOCOLATE AND MINT!

Sandy (equally angry): I UNDERSTAND THE FLAVOR, I DON'T KNOW WHY YOU ARE EATING CHAPSTICK!

Larry: Who's eating Chapstick?

Steve: Stop...these are two different conversation...Dad is eating candy from the boys and you are using Chapstick.

Larry: Do they have chocolate and mint Chapstick?

As soon as I got back to the office, I quickly typed out a transcript of what happened and sent it to Amy, Cat, Kelly and my parents. The story itself is so surreal and funny, mostly because it's so unbelievably true, that the hilarity grew as the recipients of my email began to share their stories of their reaction as they read it.

Amy was the first to react saying she felt really awkward laughing like crazy in the middle of her office as she read it. My sister actually snorted at a business luncheon as she read it on her phone. My mom howled with laughter so hard, Akester came running in the room to see if she was okay. She couldn't even speak because she was laughing and crying. Your typical teenager, my daughter Cat just wondered if we should look into a home for them.

Epilogue Part II

In the eight days after *The Chapstick* story, we must have laughed and relived that story a 100 times, with dad toggling back-and-forth between trying to defend himself and just laughing along with us. A heart attack on 12-12-12 didn't rob us of more stories, it robbed us of a husband, a father and a grandfather.

While there isn't a day that has gone by I haven't thought of him and missed him, I can still look back on these stories and laugh.

I hope you got a laugh out of them too!

12-12-12

Conclusion

Our family cherishes the story of my father shared here along with the funny stories from his life. Laughter was always a central theme for our family so it is great to be able to share them with so many others via this book.

In the months after his death, we saw many things we attributed to signs from my dad. The first for me was when my mom thought it might be a good idea to bring his beloved iPad to his wake so we could set it up and play the songs he downloaded. After all, this was the music he liked. What better tribute than having his songs playing that we could share them with his friends and family.

When I turned on the music, hit the button to set up a random song, Bruce Springsteen's *Further on up the Road* began playing. It was almost haunting to hear Bruce singing about a dead man and the chorus repeated again-and-again, "I'll see you further on up the road."

My mom and I would share stories about the weird places we were finding pennies. Was the penny where we store our Christmas tree a sign from dad that he was with us for Christmas? What about the ones we found at the Super Bowl party? He loved hosting the Super Bowl party. Was he there too?

I don't know if you believe in that kind of stuff. Heck, I don't know if I believe in that kind of stuff. The truth is I don't need a psychologist or a scientist explaining to me what they think is happening with these "messages." We just take them for what they are and that's all there is to it. If they truly are a message from dad, great. If they are just random occurrences as a grieving mind tries to connect it together to make sense of a difficult situation, we're good with that too.

Nothing gave out family more comfort, though, than a dream Cat had shortly after our first Christmas without my father. She woke up at 5:38 a.m. and immediately transcribed it. The message that dad was doing okay and he looked at his life on Earth as a "dream life" really meant the world to us. I would like to conclude this book with Cat's dream from that day, as she transcribed it that morning.

From the subconscious of Cat Akley
Her dream on December 28, 2012

The dream starts out with me sitting in the passenger seat of Pa's Lexus. All of a sudden Pa gets in the driver's seat and begins to drive.

Cat: "Grandpa!"

Pa: [smiles].

[The conversation begins and progresses to this point]:

Cat: "So do you know what happened?"

Pa: "Not really…"

Cat: "…You passed away Wednesday, December 12, 2012."

Pa: "Oh."

Cat: "Were you feeling sick?"

Pa: "Well I feel a lot better now than I was then…[pauses] I can remember feeling tight-chested (he reached up and put his hand over his heart)."

[The conversation changes up again].

Pa: "So have you been driving a lot since I've been gone? Are you driving yourself to the funeral tomorrow?"

Cat: "No, but I have been driving some in these past couple weeks."

Pa: "Oh it's been that long?"

Cat: "Yes... do you not get to know the time in heaven?"

Pa: "Well we do, but it's in our 'dream life.'"

Cat: "'Dream life'"

Pa: "Yeah once you go to heaven you get to pick a dream life that you get to live."

Cat: "So what did you choose?"

Pa: "I continued my life as it was normally, because I was living the dream life."

Photo Album
A few fun photos of Dad

Crash Landing

Oh yeah, he was funny!
I mean honestly, who sleeps like this?

Helmet Head

Is anyone else wondering if he is covering up a bowtie?

Sleeping… Happy

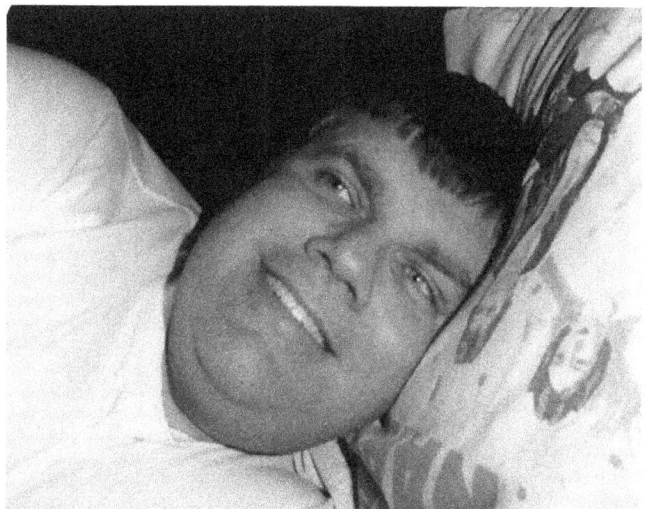

"Life is great. I got my Star Wars pillowcase and I just heard I landed the part of the giant at the repertory theater!"

Sleeping... Not Happy

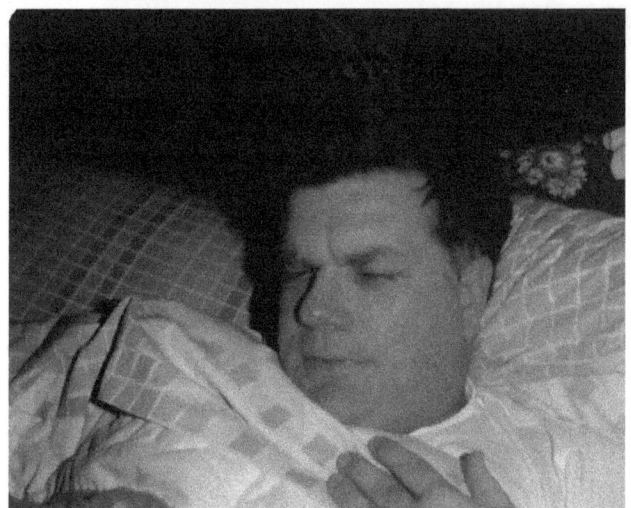

"Larry need coffee...fast...you get!"

Nothing Strange Here

This wouldn't be so bad if…

Now it's Getting Weird

...we didn't have this one too!

The Dallas Years

The TV show Dallas had a deep impact on my parents (notice Mom's Rawlings hat from the shopping adventure Dad I had).

The Holiday Face

No, it's not the bad wallpaper, or use of Jell-O molds as décor; this is the face my Dad sported during the holidays. He wasn't going to let a foul mood interfere with hair care though… the hair had to be perfect even if he was registering bah-humbug on the Christmas Cheer Meter.

Christmas '84

This goes beyond the "holiday face". This is a man with a son wearing a cardigan getting an Indiana Jones hat for Christmas while sitting with a cat wearing a t-shirt in his lap. Here is a self-evaluation of one's own life in this photo.

Just Chillin'

Is he sitting, or is that chair swallowing him?

Author's Notes

Writing this book was definitely a labor of love. I have enjoyed sharing the story of, and stories about, my father. In some ways it has seemed therapeutic to go through the process of getting my thoughts together in regard to dealing with his death.

Along the way, I had some great experiences which I truly will never forget. The shows were so incredible, but there is much more than just awesome rock shows which came out of the journey I went through writing this book.

Getting to speak to Joe Edwards of Blueberry Hill was an honor. Heroes come in all different shapes and forms. There are role models, like our parents. There are those who take care of our safety and well-being. The military, the police, paramedics and firefighters fall under this category. Celebrities, whether it be from the world of sports or entertainment, often are noted as heroes as well.

Joe Edwards is a different kind of hero. He is a local icon who has made the area where he lives and works a better place. Business savvy and acumen have ensured each step of the way, he's been successful. He doesn't sit back and enjoy the fruits of his labor, though. He turns around and leverages his new successes into his next project. The tale of Joe and his wife Linda is truly a great "only in America" story.

Of course, when you see someone in the media who is highly successful, you often have to realize their public persona, and private, can be very different. When I started this book, I had the awkward moment of trying to convey the fact I was writing a book about my father, his death, a couple of shows at the Duck room, and I would be writing about the history of Blueberry Hill as well.

I'm not sure how that comes across in an email, but I sent it asking for some information about Blueberry Hill. I got an immediate response saying Joe would answer my questions, but it would be easier to call him and get my answers over the phone.

I quickly called Blueberry Hill and spoke to Joe. The guy couldn't have been nicer. He answered every question and wished me good luck with the book. He was already off the charts in terms of respect I had for him, now it's out of the galaxy. I truly wish him the best in all current and future endeavors.

Another great experience which came out of writing this book was working with Dick and Lana Dale. Not only did I get to meet them, but also I got some keen insights into what they are like on a personal level. I knew that they are hands-on in managing their own website, so I also sent some questions their way in preparation for the book. I was thrilled when Lana responded. She shared a lot of great insight about her life and love for Dick. Their relationship seems incredible and I wish them good luck and continued good health in the future.

Just great classy people!

*My "Frankenstein Beast" Drawing
is now signed by Dick Dale*

On a personal basis, while I continue to miss my father every day, I have continued to follow the path of enjoying life again. I added a third legend to the mix by seeing a Bob Dylan show when he came to town as well. It was also a surreal experience to see him playing live. His band was great, and it was also a very special evening, in particular because Amy and I took Cat to the show. I am not sure she appreciates it as much now as she will down the road when she realizes she got to see one of the all-time greats live in concert.

Knowing that losing my father to a heart attack means that I am susceptible to the same issues, I've tried to improve my overall health. On May 12, 2013, Mother's Day, I signed up for a half-marathon with my daughter Cat. I've done many 5K races, but this race was 10 miles longer than any race I've participated in the past. Since I am not a runner, I had the added pressure of coming in ahead of the hard stop at 3 ½ hours.

I realize that beating a 15 minute per mile pace sounds ridiculous to even a non-serious runner. Those people aren't a 45-year-old, out of shape individual with a surgically repaired knee who has never participated in anything longer than a 5K though. For me, that 3 ½ hour cutoff seemed very daunting.

I'm pleased to say I completed the race ahead of its conclusion, and it was an incredibly poignant moment to have my wife Amy embrace her daughter, and me embrace my mom at the end of this Mother's Day race.

Yes, someone was missing from this special moment, but this is our new normal, and we're going to be okay.

Meeting our moms at the finish: My wife Amy, my daughter Cat, me and my mom (Sandy)

Index

*Notable individual appearances in this book (**bold** = **photo**):*

The Beast (Dick Dale's Guitar)
65 – 67 (**66**), **72**, **139**

Chuck Berry
23 – 26, 29, **39**, 43 – 55 (**46, 47, 51**), 63, 69, 71

Eric Clapton
19, 59

Dick Dale
19, 30, 44, 54 – 67, 69, 71, 138 - 139

Jimmy Dale
61

Lana Dale
65 – 67, 138

Duran Duran
28

Joe Edwards
26 – 29, **32**, **39**, 40, 42, 46, 63, 137 - 138

Linda Edwards
137

John Entwistle
18

Grandmaster Flash
28

Flea
18

Jimi Hendrix
19, 44, 60, 61, 65

Jewel
28

B.B. King
19

Lee Majors
78

Alanis Morisette
28

Joe Perry
28

Bruce Springsteen
124

Donald Trump
26

Bob Uecker
105 - 107

Stevie Ray Vaughn
19

Bonus Content

Steve's Picks for the Ultimate Chuck Berry Anthology

Two dozen must have Chuck Berry Songs

Around and Around

Back in the U.S.A.

Blues for Hawaiians

Brown Eyed Handsome Man

Jambalaya

Johnny B. Goode

Maybellene

Memphis, Tennessee

Nadine

My Ding-A-Ling

No Particular Place to Go

Reelin' and Rockin'

Rock and Roll Music

Roll Over Beethoven

Roly Poly (sometimes listed as "Rolli Polli")

Route 66

School Day (Ring Ring Goes the Bell)

Sweet Little Sixteen

Thirty Days

Too Much Monkey Business

Wee Wee Hours

Woodpecker

You Can't Catch Me

You Never Can Tell

"Bonus, Bonus" (extras above and beyond the two-dozen "must haves")
Many artists have tried, but nobody does a better version of *Run Rudolph Run* than Chuck Berry. No Christmas collection is complete without it!

Steve's Picks for the Ultimate Dick Dale Anthology

Two dozen must have Dick Dale Songs

50 Miles to Go

Banzai Washout

Esperanza

Gypsy Fire

Hava Naglia

Let's Go Trippin'

Miserlou (sometimes spelled Misrilou)

Misirlou Twist

Mr. Eliminator

Nitro

Peppermint Man

Peter Gunn

Pipeline (duet with Stevie Ray Vaughn)

Riders in the Sky

Ring of Fire

Scalped

Surf Beat

Surf Buggy

Surfing Drums

Taco Wagon

Terra Dicktyl

Third Stone from the Sun

The Victor

The Wedge

"Bonus, Bonus" (extras above and beyond the two-dozen "must haves")
If you want to add an unbelievable Christmas song to your playlist, be sure to check out Dick Dale's version of *Silent Night*.

If you would like to hear a traditional version of *Miserlou*, be sure to check out the untitled hidden track on Dick's *Tribal Thunder* album.

Special Thanks

To my mom, Sandy Akley, for her help in editing this book.

Thanks to my wife Amy for her support and love.

Thanks to my daughter Cat, for just being herself!

Hats off to my good friend Mark Hansen (*mappersmark@gmail.com*) for the great cover design. He's the greatest graphic artist you will ever find.

I really appreciated Joe Edwards taking time out of his schedule to talk with me about the Duck Room and the history of his business.

Thanks to Becca Schock of Blueberry Hill for setting up my interview with Joe.

Thanks to Lana Dale for talking candidly about her love and life with her husband Dick Dale.

Thank you to Mr. Malcom Wiseman, attorney for the Dales, for providing me with guidance on proceeding with the book.

Thanks to my buddy Darin Hansen for his graphic design skills in isolating my dad's photo in the cadet uniform which opens the book. He pulled it out of a brochure my dad appeared in promoting the department's cadet program.

Of course, I would be remiss if I didn't give props to both Chuck Berry and Dick Dale for putting on two of the best live performances I have ever seen… watching legends perform in the setting of the Duck Room was an awesome experience I will never forget!

Lastly, lots of love for my father, Larry Akley. He's always with us in spirit.

Bibliography/Sources

Akley, Cat. "*The Ultimate Life.*" Cat's dream about her grandfather. Reprinted with permission.

Blueberry Hill website: *blueberryhill.com*

Callahan, Mike and Edwards, David. "*The Chess Story.*" bsnpubs.com/chess/chesscheck.html: November 4, 2005.

Deuce of Clubs. "*Dick Dale, King of Surf Guitar.*" Planet Magazine 1995: September 26.

Interview with Blueberry Hill owner Joe Edwards: March 13, 2013

Miller, Jay N. "*Guitarist Dick Dale Dubbed the 'Cancer Warrior'.*" GateHouse News Service. October 14, 2011.

Porter, James and Austen, Jake. "*The Really Bitching Tale of Dick Dale as Told by the Man Himself.*" Rocktober 1994: Issue #8.

Schmidt, Martin. "*Interview: Dick Dale.*" Guitar Nine Records website (*www.guitar9.com*) 2004: February.

Internet Movie Database – *imdb.com*

Photographs provided by Joe Edwards/Blueberry Hill:
Exterior of Blueberry Hill, the Delmar Loop logo, the Duck Room, Blueberry Hill logo, Joe Edwards, Blueberry Hill burger, the Piano Room, the Pacman Room, the St. Louis Room, Pez collection, Elvis memorabilia, Joe Edwards and Chuck Berry, photos of Joe Edwards other properties (Tivoli, Pageant, Pin-Up Bowl and Moonrise Hotel), the logos on the timeline, the Loop Trolley, Chuck Berry statue, Chuck Berry star and the photo of Chuck Berry on stage at the Duck Room

Photographs provided by Steve Akley:
Larry Akley at Old Faithful, Crash Landing, Helmet Head, Sleeping… Happy, Sleeping… Not Happy, Nothing Strange Here,

Bibliography/Sources (continued)

Now It's Getting Weird, The Dallas Years, The Holiday Face, Christmas '84, Just Chillin' and Meeting our Moms at the Finish Line

Photographs provided by Sandy Akley:
Larry Akley in St. Louis Metropolitan Police Department (cadet uniform), Buddies for Life, "Cowboy Larry" and Larry in pajamas

Additional Resources

To follow the latest news or tour information on Chuck Berry or Dick Dale, be sure to check out their official websites:

Chuck Berry – *chuckberry.com*

Dick Dale – *dickdale.com*

If you are in the St. Louis area, be sure to head to the Delmar Loop at grab a bite or show at Blueberry Hill (6504 Delmar Boulevard, St. Louis, MO 63130). Be sure to visit their website to see who is coming to the Duck Room: *blueberryhill.com*.

In Loving Memory of Larry Akley
1942 – 2012

Dad's badge photo compliments of Kelly Brooks (thanks sis!)

About the Author

Steve Akley is a lifelong St. Louis resident. He lives with his wife Amy, their daughter Cat and a 20 lb. Maine Coon cat named Leo.

The family enjoys travel, watching NFL football and spending weekends at their second home; a log cabin in a lake community about an hour south of their home.

Steve reports that the entire family shares in his grief over the loss of his Dad, but they all cherish the funny stories and good times they had together. He also reports that everyone in the family loves ice cream.

Sign up for his newsletter, or check out his latest work, on his website: *steveakley.com*.

Steve can be reached via email: *info@steveakley.com*

Steve has a blog called *Write Steve Write!* You can read his latest posts at: *http://steveakley.wordpress.com*

Follow him on Twitter: @steveakley

Meet Team Akley

I quickly found it takes more than just an author to publish a book. Here's a look at the team that supports my efforts:

Sandy Akley/Mom
Responsibilities: Book editing, guerilla marketing, conventional marketing, grassroots marketing, local p.r. and team cheerleader

Amy Akley/Wife
Responsibilities: Mailroom, guerilla marketing and taxes

Cat Akley/Daughter
Responsibilities: Social media and guerilla marketing

Kelly Brooks/Sister, Nathan Brooks/Nephew, Mason Brooks/Nephew, Pierce Lojkovic/Nephew, Greyson Lojkovic/Nephew, Tessa Sciuto/Niece, Debbie Zebas/Aunt, Lee Ann Sciuto/Sister-in-Law
Responsibility: Guerilla marketing

Larry Akley/Father
Responsibility: Inspiration

Also by Steve Akley

Christmas is the best time of the year, why settle for anything less than the best holiday music? *The 101 Best Christmas Songs* is designed to assist you in creating the ultimate playlist by focusing on the best versions of Christmas favorites.

Leo the Coffee Drinking Cat is a children's book which highlights the special bond between a talking/coffee drinking cat and his 3 year-old owner Catherine. When Leo tells her he dreams of visiting the coffee paradise of Starbucks, it's up to Catherine to get him there.

To learn more, and to sign-up for a mailing list so you know when Steve's latest book is out, check out:
www.steveakley.com

Read his blog at: **http://steveakley.wordpress.com**

Follow him on Twitter:

@steveakley

In Loving Memory of Larry Akley

Son, Brother, Husband, Brother-in-Law, Father, Uncle, Father-in-Law, Grandfather, Policeman's Policeman and Friend to All!

www.ingramcontent.com/pod-product-compliance
Lightning Source LLC
Chambersburg PA
CBHW071508040426
42444CB00008B/1545